Adobe Photoshop™
A Visual Guide for the Mac

*A step-by-step approach
to learning imaging software*

Bert Monroy and David Biedny

Addison-Wesley Publishing Company

Reading, Massachusetts • Menlo Park, California • New York
Don Mills, Ontario • Wokingham, England • Amsterdam
Bonn • Sydney • Singapore • Tokyo • Madrid • San Juan
Paris • Seoul • Milan • Mexico City • Taipei

Library of Congress Cataloging-in-Publication Data has been applied for.

ISBN 0-201-48993-7

Cover design by Zofia T. Rostomian
Book design by Zofia T. Rostomian and Bert Monroy
Set in Garamond Light Condensed and Franklin Gothic Condensed
by Zofia T. Rostomian and Bert Monroy

Manufacturing in Hong Kong
First printing, 1995

Addison-Wesley books are available for bulk purchases by corporations, institutions, and other organizations. For more information about how to make such purchases in the United States, please contact the Corporate, Government, and Special Sales Department at 1-800-238-9682.

Dedication

To my wife, Zosia, for many years of encouragement, support and fun.
B.M.

To Felicity Biedny and Anna "Oma" Reinfeld.
D.B.

Acknowledgements

We wish to thank those individuals who provided help and support in the preparation of this book. They, Zosia T. Rostomian, Nathan Moody, Hellene Biedny, Eric Reinfeld and Frank Colin shared their time and expertise. Jody Sprague for incredible proofreading.

We would also like to thank the folks at Adobe, Patricia Pane, Sara Daley, John Leddy, Mark Hamburg, Luanne Cohen and all the rest, for providing us and the world with a great tool to work with and write about. Special thanks to that great all around guy Russell Brown for sharing some of his tips in the book. Additional thanks go to those two brothers that started this whole thing—John and Tom Knoll.

Additional thanks go to the gang at Cantoo, Inc. in Berkeley for helping out with the occasional emergency. All the students we've had through the years who have taught us how to explain things properly also deserve some thanks.

Special thanks go to our families for putting up with us. Zosia, Hellene, Erika and Sean provided support and the distractions to keep us going.

Finally, we want to thank each other. We're friends and neighbors and always manage to get the job done.

Bert Monroy and David Biedny

Contents

How to Use This Book   **1**
1   Photoshop Basics 2
2   Optimized Performance 6

Tools
3   Cloning 10
4   Colorizing Grayscale 13
5   Transparency Effect 16

Filters
6   Instant Textures from Scratch 21
7   Water Reflection 24
8   Lens Flare 30
9   Lighting Effects Filter 32

Alpha Channels
10   Alpha Channels 38
11   Rings on a Planet 43
12   Cut-out Effect 46
13   Creating a Grid 50
14   Selecting Hair 54

Working with Adobe Illustrator
15   Creating Templates for Illustrator 58
16   Patterns and Masks 62
17   Edge Enhancement 66

Layers
18   Working with Layers 68
19   Rainbow Blend 72
20   Retouching with Layers 75
21   Drop Shadows Using Layers 80
22   Complex Shadows Using Layers 82
23   Global Layer Adjustments 86
24   Wet Glass Effect 88

©Bert Monroy '92

Formats 124
Glossary 127
Shortcuts/Resources 135
Index 136
About the Authors 138

Working with Color

25 Color Correction 89
26 Overexposure, Correction with Layers 92
27 Variations 93

Tips and Techniques

28 Interactive Inline Type 96
29 Metallic Type 98
30 Soft 3D Type Embossing 103
31 Quick and Easy 3D Buttons 106
32 Glory Shot 110
33 Painting 118

How To Use This Book

Pictures tell the story and this book has many stories to tell. Here are some tips on how to best navigate through the information.

- Tools
- Filters
- Alpha Channels
- Layers
- Color

Retouching with Layers

Painting

Covering the subject
Photoshop is one of the most powerful and complex programs available today. This book is presented in a step-by-step fashion with images and clear explanations for each step. Chapter 1 covers how to optimize the performance of Photoshop.

Presenting functionality
The subsequent chapters demonstrate specific features of Photoshop. In most cases, various functions are outlined within a specific task. All chapters read page by page and not across a 2-page spread.

Describing real-world projects
Other chapters guide you through the steps taken to solve specific problems that come up in the preparation of finished artwork. The finished art is shown in the title block of the chapter.

6. Option-Command-T is pressed again. This time with the Lasso tool and the Command key pressed to deselect, the lower portion of the selected type, which was filled with the blend, is surrounded to subtract it from the selection.

1	Speed Optimization	2
Tools		
2	Cloning	6
3	Colorizing	9
4	Transparency	12
Filters		
5	Water Effect	17
6	Lens Flare	23
7	Lighting Effects	25
8	Texture Color Noise	31
Alpha Channels		
9	Alpha Channels	34

C
calculations Photoshop operations which compare the pixels of two images and apply discrete logic testing to yield a resulting set of pixels.

calibration The process of equalizing and balancing the color values of different steps of a production process, including scanning, display and output devices.

calibration bars A set of swatches on the side of a printed image to denote the 11-step

Showing and telling
In both the technique and projects chapters, the how-to descriptions are highly illustrated, with easy to follow instructions for each step in the process being covered. *This symbol signals useful tips and shortcuts.*

Using the table of contents
The projects and techniques are grouped within sections of the book, according to topic. The project number is listed on the left with the page number on the right.

Glossary
In the back of the book is one of the most complete glossaries you will find, which covers not only image processing but computers in general.

Browsing
Because the book is highly visual, one way to locate a specific technique—or just to find inspiration or a jumping-off point for your own exploration—is to flip the pages of the book and look at the pictures. We hope you will enjoy the book as well as find it useful.

1

Photoshop Basics

Version 3.0 of Photoshop introduced many new features. Among them was a series of enhancements to the interface to lessen the complexity of the program's functions.

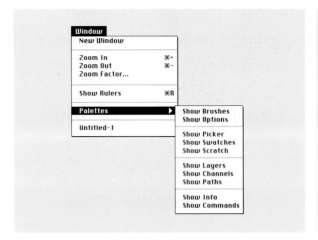

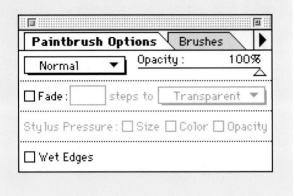

1. Show palettes

All options and size dialog boxes for the tools as well as the color selection palettes and other useful functions can remain visible at all times. They are summoned through the Palettes sub menu of the Windows menu.

2. Working with palettes

These palettes have tabs to switch from one function to the other. Here we see the Brush Options palette with the tab for the sizes visible behind it.

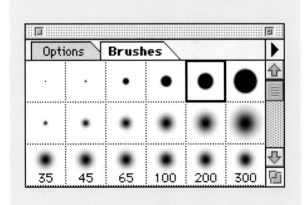

Clicking on the tab will bring that palette to the forefront.

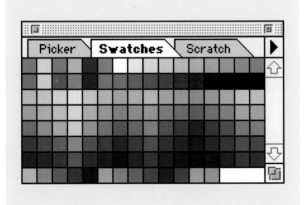

There are times when you might want to have all the palettes visible. Here we see the Colors palette.

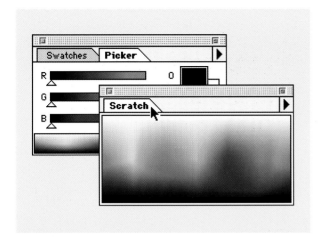

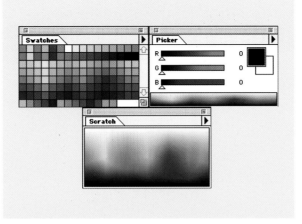

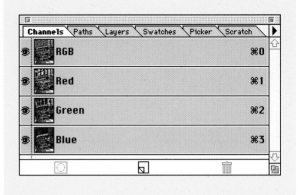

Grabbing the tab and pulling it out of the main window will give it its own palette. Here we see the Scratch portion of the colors palette being separated.

Above we see all the palettes which make up color selection separated into individual palettes.

Of course, this could lead to a very crowded screen. The opposite can also be done. Palettes can be combined to form a single palette with many tabs. To combine palettes you simply drag tabs over other palettes and they will combine. Above we see such a combination.

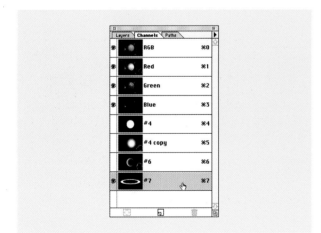

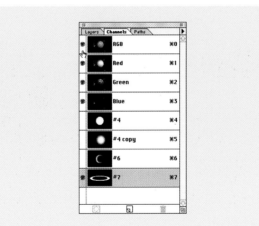

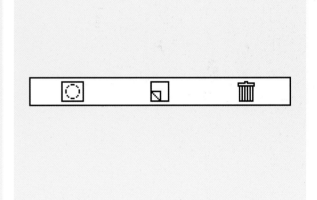

3. Channels palette
The palettes for the Alpha channels, Layers and Path tool have built-in features to simplify the operation of these functions. The Channels palette displays all available channels. Clicking on any of the channels will make that channel active for writing to.

Clicking on the Eye icon in the panel to the left of the channel will allow you to see the channels.

The three icons at the bottom of the palette simplify the functionality of the channels. Dragging a channel over the icon at the far left will make that channel a selection. Dragging a channel over the center icon will make a duplicate channel. Dragging a channel over the Trash icon will delete it.

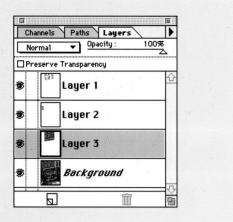

4. Layers palette

The Layers palette is similar to the Channels palette with some additions. At the top of the palette, the opacity of the layer can be controlled.

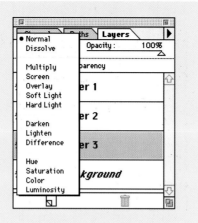

The Modes for the layers are also found at the top of the palette.

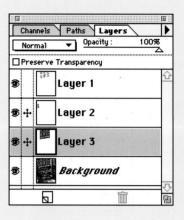

There is a panel between the eye panel and the layer name. Clicking in this panel will link layers to each other so that when one is moved, the linked ones will move with it.

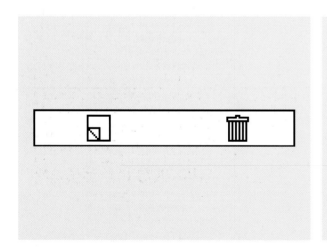

There are only two icons at the bottom of the Layers palette. Dragging a layer over the Document icon at the left will make a duplicate of the layer. Dragging a layer over the Trash icon will delete it.

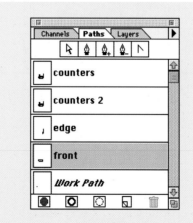

5. Paths palette

The Paths tool palette has all the tool variations at the top. Like the Channels and Layers palette, clicking on a saved path will make it active.

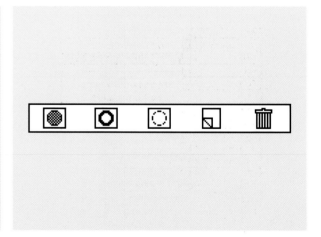

There are five icons at the bottom of the Path palette. Dragging a path over the first one will fill the contents of the path with the foreground color. The second icon will stroke the path.  *When stroking the path, whichever tool is currently chosen will be the tool used to create the stroke.* Dragging a path over the center icon will make it a selection. Dragging a path over the Document icon will make a duplicate. Finally, dragging a path over the Trash icon will delete it.

6. Commands palette

Often-used commands can be executed through the new Commands palette. This comes in handy for sub menu commands. You just click on the desired command.

To add a command to the list, you choose New Command from the Palettes menu.

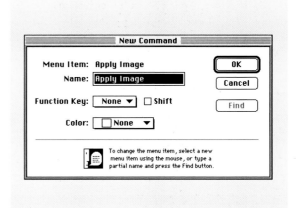

In the dialog box which pops up you simply go to the menu choice and it will appear in the Name box. A function key can be assigned. A color can also be given to distinguish different sets of commands.

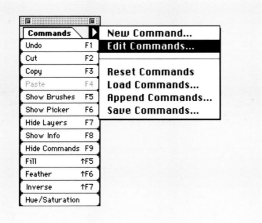

To minimize the amount of room occupied by the Commands palette you can customize the way in which the commands are listed. Choose Edit Commands from the Commands palette menu.

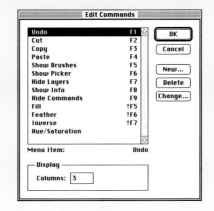

In the dialog box that appears, various functions can be performed including the number of columns used to display the commands.

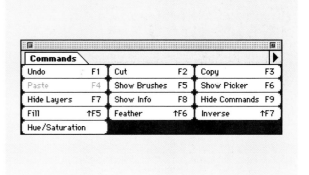

The result is a more efficient use of space.

2

Optimized Performance

Photoshop is one of the most processor and memory hungry programs that you'll ever use on your computer. There are some steps which you can take to ensure that Photoshop will run as fast as possible on your system.

Scratch Disk Setup

1. Photoshop 3.0 is designed to run on both the Macintosh 68000 and PowerPC processors, but the fact is that the program has been optimized to deliver faster relative performance on the PowerPC processor.

2. Photoshop will always perform faster if images can be contained totally within RAM memory. You'll want as much memory as you can feasibly afford, especially if you plan on working with prepress resolution images. Allocate up to 90% of your available RAM (but no more) to Photoshop, by adjusting memory allocation in the Get Info dialog of the Photoshop application. To do this, select Photoshop in the Finder and choose the Get Info command from the File menu. The important field here is Preferred size; in this example (**A**), 35 megabytes have been allocated to Photoshop.

3. The scratch disk (which Photoshop uses to buffer current image information) should be your fastest fixed hard drive. Even though you might be tempted to use removable media (such as Syquest and magneto-optical (MO) cartridges), DON'T! These types of storage media are designed for burst data transfers, NOT sustained data throughput. Scratch disks are specified by selecting File>Preferences> Scratch Disks (sample **B**). The primary drive is the main scratch disk, while the secondary handles overflow if the first scratch disk fills up (sample **C**).

4. While any fixed hard drive is a good scratch disk, you'll see even better overall performance if you designate a disk array as a scratch disk. This technique essentially uses multiple hard drives to emulate one big hard drive, which has the effect of boosting access and throughput speeds rather significantly (especially if the drives stripped together into an array all have decent performance specifications). There are a number of hardware and software products to create your own array; adding a SCSI-2 Fast and/or Wide NUBUS or PCI board (such as the FWB Jackhammer) will make the array even faster.

A
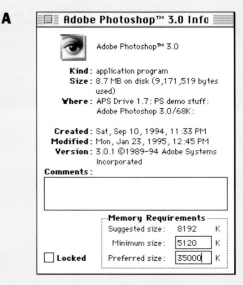

B

C
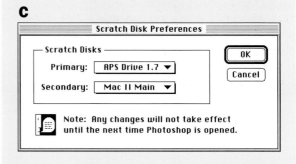

5. If you decide to create a disk array using a software-only solution (such as the Remus array software from Trillium Research Inc.), consider getting a Macintosh model with built-in dual SCSI busses. Currently, the Quadra 950 and Power Macintosh 8100 series machines offer dual SCSI capabilities, and will deliver the best results with a software-based drive array. You'll need to use a combination of internal and external hard drives in order to use both SCSI ports.

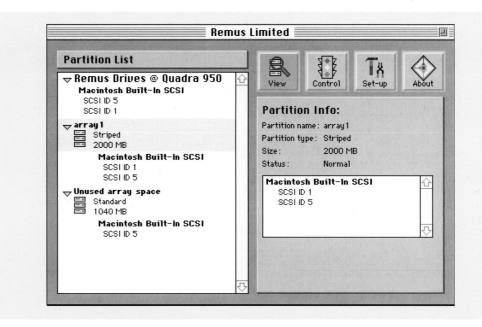

Memory

6. The settings in the memory control panel will have a direct effect on Photoshop. You'll want to make sure that your Disk Cache is set to the lowest possible number (32K), though one of the Photoshop programmers, Mark Hamburg, recommends setting the Disk Cache to 96K. On 68K Macs, the Virtual Memory should always be set to off; Power Macintosh models can be used successfully with small virtual memory allocations, if you're truly strapped for RAM. If you decide to use virtual memory with your Power Mac, always make sure that the amount of memory specified in Virtual Memory is never more than the actual amount of physical RAM in your machine. For example, if your Power Mac has 32 megabytes of RAM, you shouldn't set virtual memory to more than 32 megabytes. And make sure that the drive specified for virtual memory is a reasonably fast hard drive (though you should try to avoid using the same drive for Photoshop's scratch file and the system's virtual memory). 32-Bit Addressing should always be turned on. If you have programs that won't run with 32-bit addressing, get updates or get rid of them.

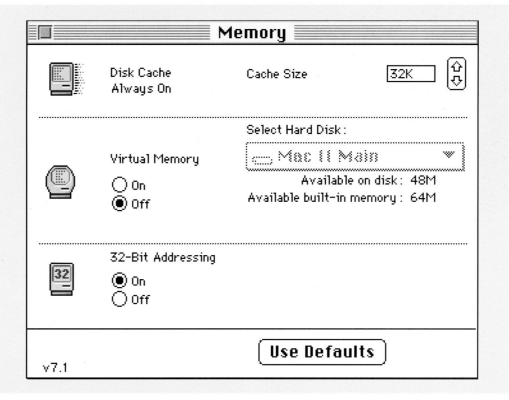

Setting up views

7. Once you've done all these steps and have launched Photoshop, there are some other things you can do to keep Photoshop running as efficiently and quickly as possible. When working with documents which contain multiple layers, consider turning off the thumbnails in the Layers palette. To do this, choose Palette Options from the popup menu in the upper right corner of the Layers palette (**A**). If you absolutely want or need these thumbnails, then choose the smallest tolerable size or None (**B**).

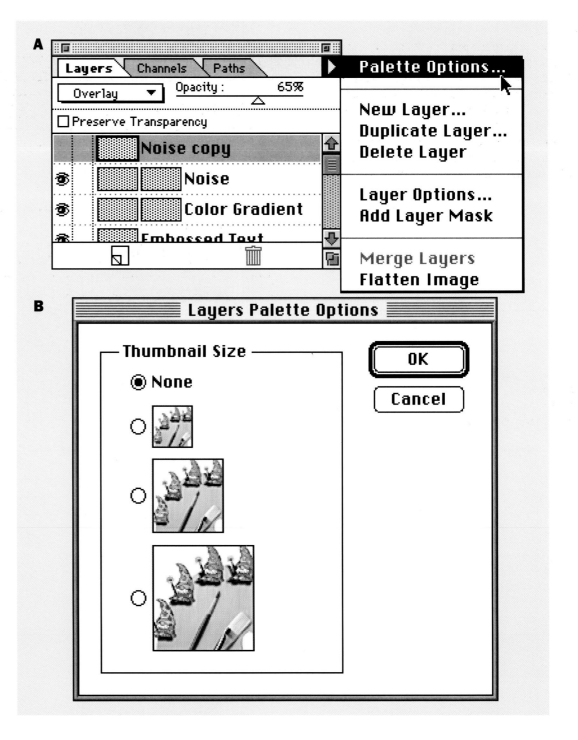

WindowShade

8. Keep as few documents open as possible. If you're done working with a specific image, then save and close it. The more documents open at a time, the slower the program will run. If you want the best of both worlds, then get a hold of the shareware CDEV called WindowShade (now a standard part of Apple system 7.5X), which reduces open documents to their title bar, and keeps Photoshop from having to redraw the document on the screen even while the document is open. WindowShade can be found in all of the major on-line services (such as America Online and Compuserve) as well as many Internet FTP sites.

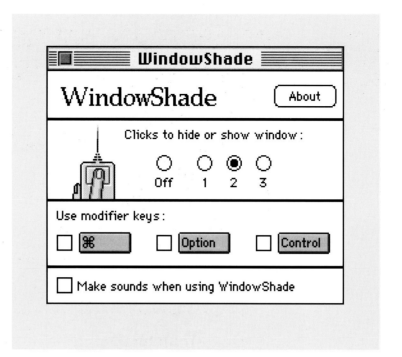

RAMDoubler

9. RAMDoubler, a cool software utility published by Connectix, Inc. should not be used with Photoshop. Under any conditions. Really.

3

Cloning

Cloning is one of the most effective methods of photo retouching. Every image has a texture, whether it is part of the image or the grain in the film. When retouching, it is necessary to maintain that texture to avoid detection.

The Rubber-stamp tool has the clone technique built into it. There are two methods, aligned and non-aligned. To use this effect you click over the area you wish to clone while holding down the Option button. The cursor is then placed over the area where the clone is to appear. When you click and drag, two cursors will be visible. The first is the one you are controlling while cloning. The other indicates the area from which you are cloning.

In Aligned, the position of the two cursors with relation to each other will remain the same. In Non-Aligned, the cursor which indicates the area being cloned from will always start from the same position regardless of where you are cloning to.

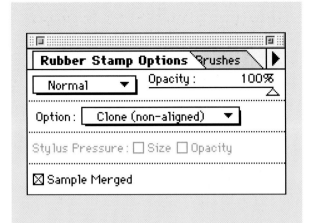

The controls in the Options window allow you to determine Opacity as well as the Mode. The size of the tool is determined in the Brushes window. At the bottom of the Options window is an option called Sample Merged. This feature allows you to work as usual but any modification to the image will be applied to a selected layer as opposed to the actual image.

The image shown above will be retouched to solve a problem. The job called for a single boat on a large body of water. The additional boats and their reflections in the water must be removed.

In this case it is very important to clone from areas of similar focus and color. Also, it is most important to clone into a large area from small areas from different parts of the image. The reason being that water is a random texture. If you clone the same area over and over, the eye will pick up the similarity.

The result will be an image which seems to be in its original form.

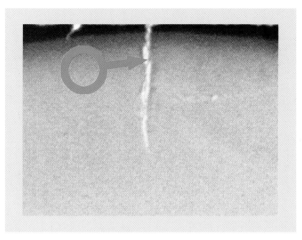

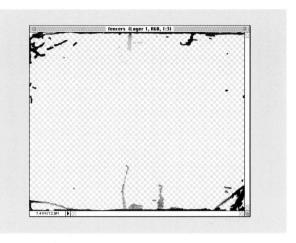

Damages to an image are removed in the same manner. In the case of the image shown here, a dramatic restoration was required. Scratches and tears had to be eliminated.

Areas in close proximity to the destroyed areas are cloned over the damage.

Since Sample Merged was selected all changes were written to a separate layer. This gives you the ability to undo sections at any time. It also gives you an accurate record of all work done if it is necessary to account for it.

The final result is a restored photograph.

Cloning can also be used to create a totally new image from parts of other images. The job called for an image of a doughnut with a bite taken out of it. We had an image of a doughnut but no bite.

When a bite is taken, the interior dough is visible. An image of a slice of bread can be used for this texture.

The first thing to do is create the bite. Using the clone tool and a circular brush size proportionally equal to a tooth, the surface on which the doughnut is sitting is cloned over the doughnut. This is done into its own layer.

The texture inside the doughnut will now be cloned from the image of the bread. 🍎 *The clone tool allows you to clone from one file to another*. With both files opened, and the doughnut as the current active file, option-click over the inactive file of the slice of bread in the background.

A new layer is created. The texture is then cloned into the area of the bite in its own layer.

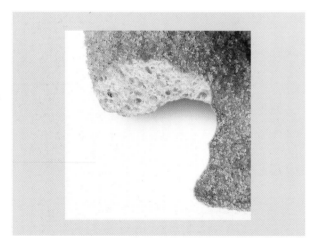

The layer with the original bite made of the background surface is made active, and using the Airbrush, a slight shadow is added to simulate the one on the outer side of the doughnut.

Finally, for that touch of realism, another file is opened which has some crumbs.

Using the same clone from the other technique used for the texture, the crumbs are cloned over to the doughnut.

4

Colorizing Grayscale

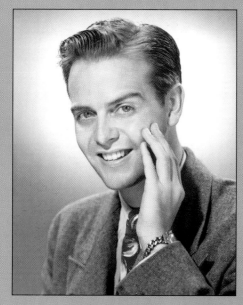

Colorizing has been very popular in the movies lately. There was a time before color film when photographs were hand tinted to show color.

There are many instances today when it is necessary to colorize a black and white photo or change the existing color.

The modes for the various tools and fills contain a mode called Color. This mode will change the hue of the pixels that are modified but leave the luminosity values intact. This means the color changes but the highlights and shadows remain the same.

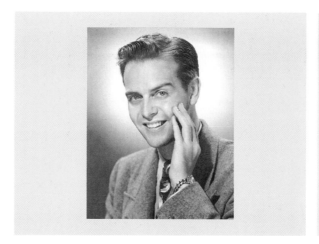

We start with an old black & white (grayscale) photo.

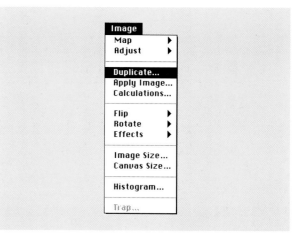

1. This file is Duplicated so we can work on a copy and not destroy the original.

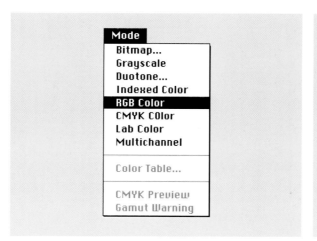

2. In order for the image to accept color, it must first be converted to RGB or CMYK. These choices can be found under the Mode menu.

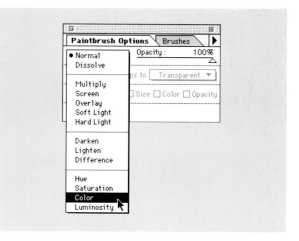

3. Double-click on the tool you wish to use to bring up its Options palette. In this case, the Paintbrush is used. In the Options palette the Mode is changed to Color.

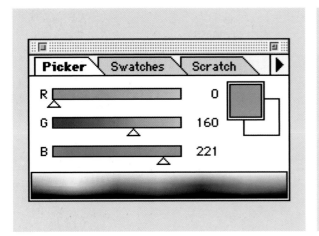

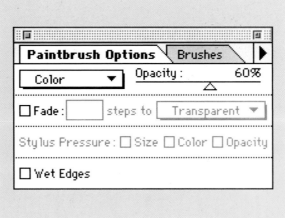

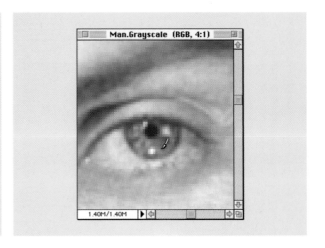

4. A color is chosen to paint with. In this case, a blue is selected for the eyes.

5. The Opacity is reduced for the brush. This will soften the effect.

6. The eye is now painted with the Color Mode Paintbrush.

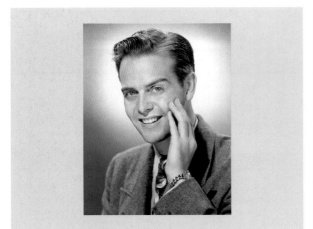

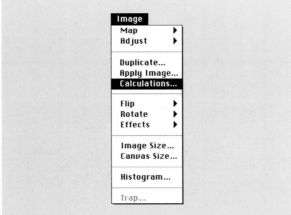

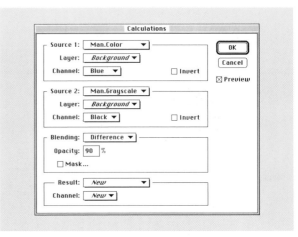

After the entire man is colored, it is necessary to colorize the background. For this situation, a particular method works well. It will not work for all situations. Refer to other chapters on Selecting in this book for additional techniques.

7. With both the colorized image and the original grayscale image opened, Calculations is chosen from the Image menu.

8. In the Calculations dialog box, the difference between the Blue channel of the color image and the grayscale image is calculated.
🍎 *Experimentation with the various channels of other images may produce a similar effect.*

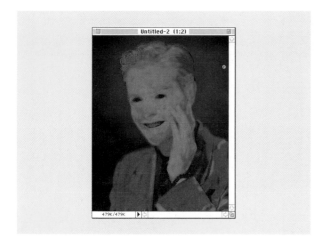

The result is the sample shown above.

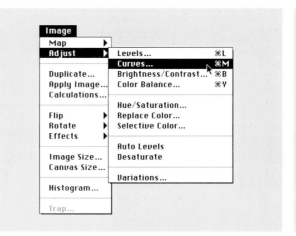

9. Curves is selected from the Adjust sub menu of the Image menu.

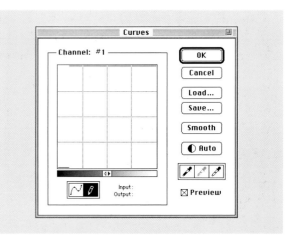

 Passing the cursor over the image will show the position of any particular color on the scale from white to black in the Curves dialog box.

10. The colors which pertain to the background are changed to black. All others (the man) are turned to white.

The result of the Curves change.

11. With the Eraser tool, the excess detail is eliminated from the man. The image is then inverted to serve as an alpha channel for the background.

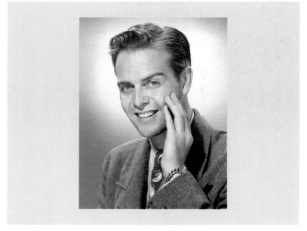

12. With the background selected, Hue/Saturation is used to colorize the background.

5

Transparency Effect

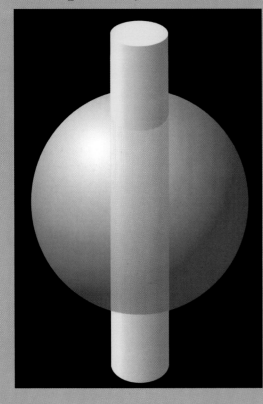

The effect of an object being transparent can be used on many different occasions. In this exercise you will create a transparent sphere with an opaque rod running through it. This particular effect has been used in many medical illustrations. The technique can be applied for other situations you might come up against. It gives you some insight into the various paste options under the Edit menu.

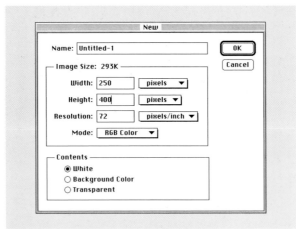

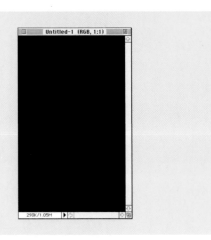

Setting up document parameters

1. Choose New from the File menu. Start a file which is 250 pixels wide by 400 pixels in height with a resolution of 72. RGB should be the Mode.

2. When the file opens, it is a blank, white canvas. For this exercise, we will work on black to add drama. Press Command-I to invert the window to black. ◆ *This is the same action as going to the Map sub menu of the Image menu and choosing Invert.*

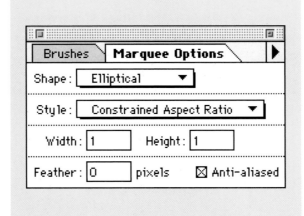

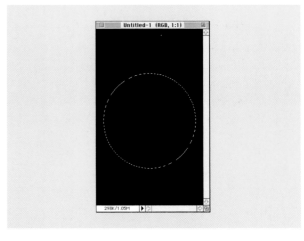

Choosing the Elliptical Marquee tool

3. In the Tools palette, go up to the Marquee tool. With the Option button pressed, click once on the tool to convert it to the Elliptical Marquee tool. Double click the Elliptical Marquee tool and the Brushes window pops up. In the section labeled Style, select the Constrained Aspect Ratio option leaving 1 to 1 as the ratio. Make sure the Feather is set to 0 and the Anti-aliased option is selected. This will allow you to select a perfect circle.

4. Place the cursor at the center of the window and with the Option button pressed, drag a circular selection similar to the one shown above. ◆ *Pressing the Option button when selecting with the Rectangle or Elliptical tools allow you to select from the center out.*

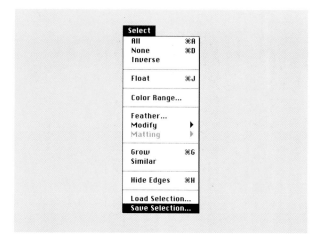

Saving a selection to an alpha channel

5. Go to the Select menu and choose Save Selection.

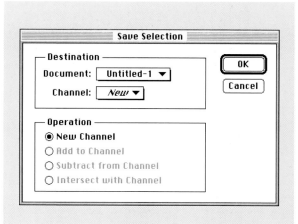

6. A dialog box pops up which allows you to determine the attributes of the alpha channel being created when the selection is saved. New Channel is the only choice in the Operation section of the window. With the settings as they are, click OK.

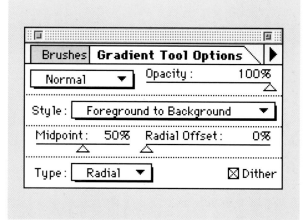

Choosing the Gradient tool

7. Double click the Gradient tool. In the Brushes window, the options for the Gradient tool will appear. Select the Radial option under Type.

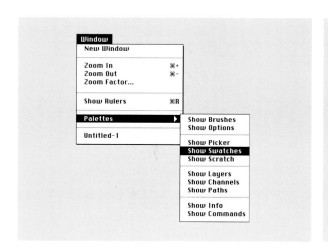

Choosing colors

8. Open your colors swatches palette by choosing Show Swatches under the Palettes sub menu of the Windows menu.

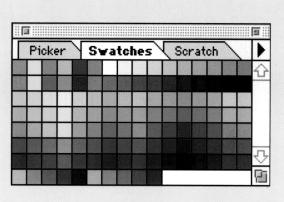

9. For the Foreground color, choose the white shade which is the seventh swatch on the upper left of the window. For the Background color, with the Option button pressed, click on the dark blue swatch which is the fifth one on the upper left. ♦ *Holding down the Option button while selecting colors will select the color for the background.*

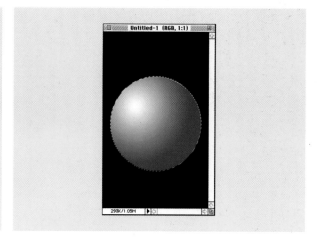

Colorizing the ball

10. Place the cursor in the upper left quadrant of the selected area and click and drag a gradient to the lower right quadrant. The result should look like this. If it doesn't, press Command-Z and do it again.

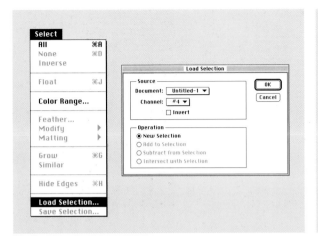

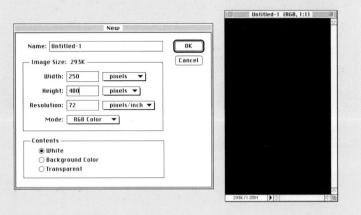

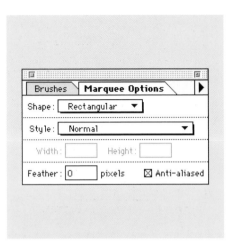

11. The circle should still be selected. If it is not, choose Load Selection from the Select menu to select the circle. A dialog box pops up which allows you to determine the attributes the selection will take. The Channel should be #4 and the Operation: New Selection.

Starting a new file

12. Start another file which is 250 pixels wide by 400 pixels in height with a resolution of 72, just as before. Press Command-I to invert the window to black.

Creating the rod

13. In the Marquee Options window, under Shape, return to Rectangular. Under Style, return to Normal.

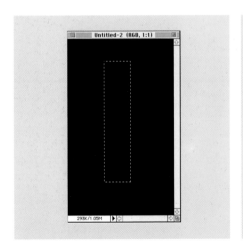

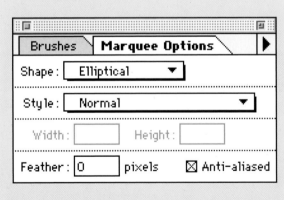

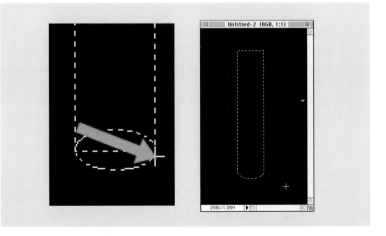

14. With the Rectangle Marquee selection tool, select a rectangle exactly like the one shown here.

15. This will be the rod that penetrates the sphere. The rod, however, is circular. To see this, it is necessary to add perspective. In the Marquee Options window, reselect the Elliptical under Shape.

16. With the Shift key pressed to add to the selection, place the cursor about a quarter of an inch up from the bottom and at the left edge of the current selection and drag down and to the right edge and just below the bottom of the selection to add a circular bottom to the rod.

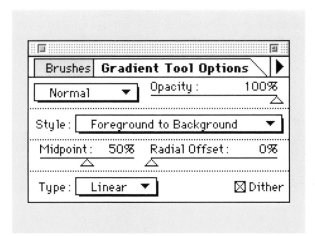

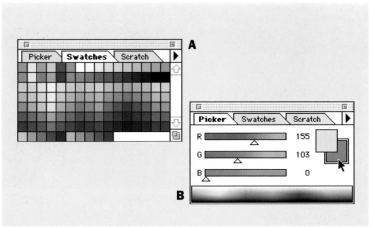

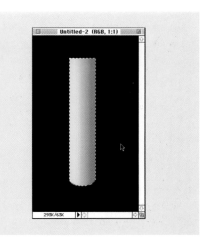

17. Double click the Gradient tool. In the Options window, go back to the Linear under Type.

18. In the Colors palette, (**A**) for the Foreground color, choose the bright yellow which is the second swatch on the upper left. For the Background color, with the Option button pressed, choose the same bright yellow. Click the tab at the top of the Colors palette window which says Picker. This will switch to that portion of the window. Click on the lower swatch on the right. Here you will darken the yellow by moving the upper and center bars as shown in (**B**).

19. Click and drag a gradient just a bit in from the left edge to just before the right edge. Go to the Select menu and choose Save Selection. Press Command-D to deselect.

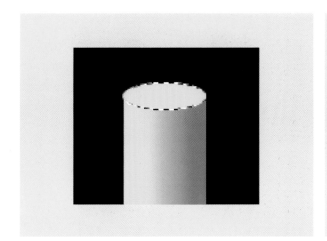

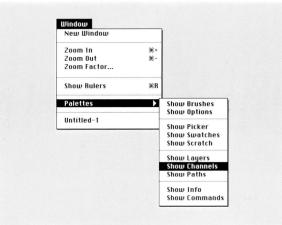

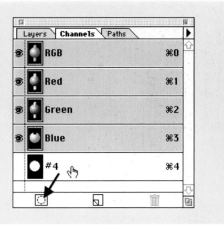

20. With the Elliptical Marquee tool, draw an oval at the top of the rod as shown. Use the edges of the rod as your guide as you did when you added the bottom of the rod, starting just above the edge. Press Option-delete to fill it with the foreground color, yellow.

21. Go to the Select menu and Load Selection. Click OK in the dialog box that pops up. Press Command-G to spread the selection to incorporate the yellow top. Press Command-C to copy to the clipboard.

Adding effect to sphere file

22. Go to the file that has the sphere. You now have to load the alpha channel as a selection. This time let's do it the easy way. Go up to the Windows menu and under Palettes, choose Show Channels.

23. You should see the alpha channel you just created visible in the Channels window. It should be called #4. In the Channels window, place the cursor over the alpha channel (#4) and click and drag it over the little icon of a box with a circle at the lower left of the Channels window. This will load the alpha channel as a selection over the RGB file.

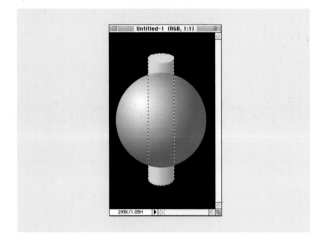

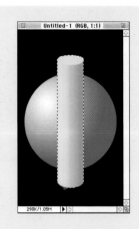

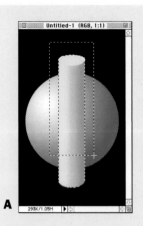

24. With the Option button pressed, choose Paste Into from the Edit menu. This will paste the rod from the clipboard behind the selected sphere. ⌘ *The Paste Behind option has been replaced in the menu by Paste Layer... and now operates with the Option key as described in this step.* You will now notice that the rod appears to be behind the ball. Do not deselect.

25. Now press Command-V to paste another copy of the rod over the one you just pasted behind the sphere. This time the rod appears directly in front of the sphere in the exact position as the previous one. ⌘ *If an area is selected, Paste from the Edit menu or Command-V will paste the contents of the clipboard centered over the selection.*

26. With the Rectangle Marquee tool and the Command button pressed to subtract from the selection, subtract the top portion of the rod. This is accomplished by dragging a rectangle over the rod as shown in Figure **A**. This will leave only the bottom portion of the rod as shown in Figure **B**. ⌘ *The Command key with any of the selection tools allows you to subtract from the selection. In this case, since the selection is a floating selection, any portion subtracted will disappear.*

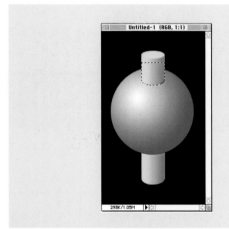

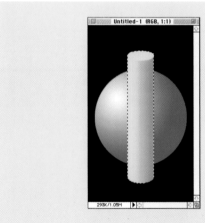

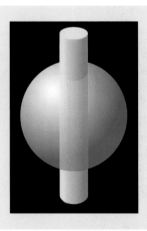

27. Move up the remaining selected portion of the rod bottom, keeping it centered within the original rod visible behind the ball, to simulate the penetration point of the rod as shown above.

28. In the Channels window place the cursor over the alpha channel (#4) and click and drag it over the little icon of a box with a circle at the lower left of the Channels window. (See step 23).

29. Choose Paste Into from the Edit menu. This pastes a copy of the rod into the circular selected area.

30. The key now is to bring down the opacity of this internal portion of the rod. Pressing the number keys on the keyboard will change the opacity of the pasted object. To use this function, make sure you have one of the selection tools selected (i.e. Lasso, Marquee, etc.). Press the 5 key for a 50% opacity, 7 for 70% etc. If you want more or less, press another number. The effect is now complete.

6

Instant Textures from Scratch

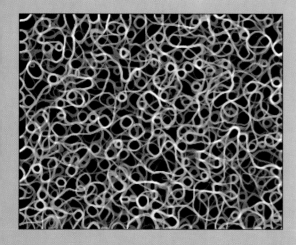

While there are a myriad of texture-making programs and texture plug-ins for Photoshop, there are often times when you find yourself sitting in front of a vanilla Photoshop, without your normal filter toolkit at hand. In such cases, it's very easy to instantly use built-in Photoshop tools to create a large variety of attractive and useful textures (for everything from backgrounds to custom fill effects). Let's look at some of the basics.

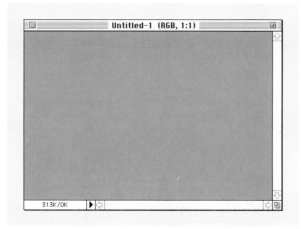

1. Very often, good textures have their foundations in nothing more complicated than some noise. Create a new RGB document, and fill it with a medium gray.

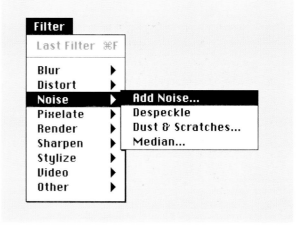

2. Select Filter>Noise>Add Noise.

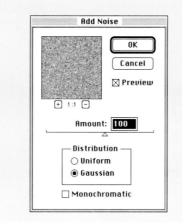

3. Choose Gaussian for Distribution, and 100 for Amount. Make sure Monochromatic is not checked (so that the noise is colored). Click OK.

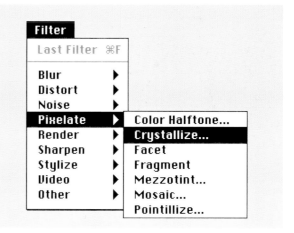

4. The next step is to "mold" the noise with another filter. For this example, we'll use the Crystallize filter (Filter>Pixelate>Crystallize).

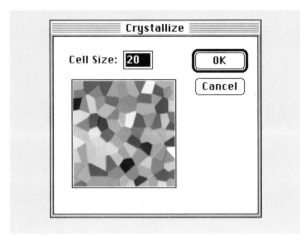

A dialog box will appear which allows you to specify a size. For this example, we'll specify a cell size of 20.

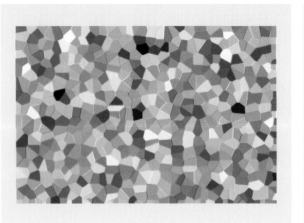

5. The results are a colorful stained-glass-looking texture.

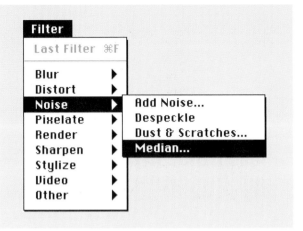

6. While this texture is ready to be used, we'll take it a step further, by "rounding" the sharp edges of the shards. In order to do this, select Filter>Noise>Median.

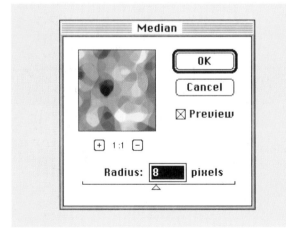

7. We'll try a Median value of 8 pixels. ❖ *Higher values will soften and blend the edges more, while lower values preserve more of the shape of each shard.*

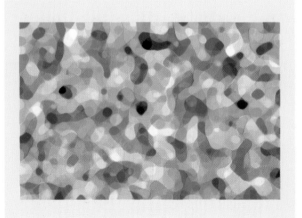

The resulting image is what we call "Psychedelic Camouflage."

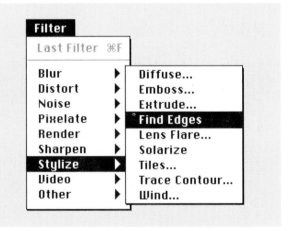

8. You can get even more variations of this already neat texture by applying other built-in filters. For example, let's apply the Find Edges filter (Filter>Stylize>Find Edges).

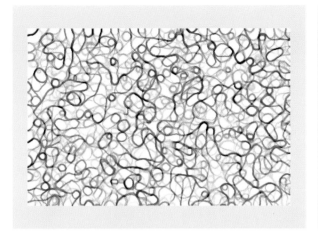

The result is striking.

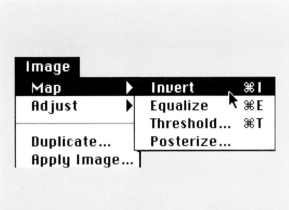

9. Finally, apply an Invert command (Image>Map>Invert).

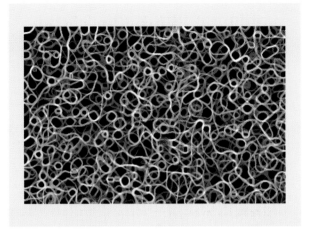

There you have it. Start with a little noise, experiment, and discover the multitude of possibilities from pushing a little noise around with filters!

The possibilities are endless! The simple fabric-like texture above started out as a gray background like the one at the beginning of this chapter. The Noise filter was added in Monochromatic mode. A Median filter was then applied and finally a Sharpen More filter.

This watery effect started with the same gray background and Monochromatic Noise. The Mezotint filter was then applied in Short Lines mode. Next, the Ripple filter was used with Medium sized ripples. Finally, the texture was colorized with the Hue/Saturation controls.

This marble-like texture starts with the same gray color, Noise and Mezotint filter as the water image. To the result, a Wave filter is applied. Next a Pinch filter. Then the Wave filter is applied again and the result is colorized. Playing with various combinations will produce astonishing results not to mention the fun in experimenting.

7

Water Reflection

Photoshop ships with many filters and many more are available from third party companies. The functions of some filters are obvious. Others require a little experimentation or reading of the documentation.

What we plan to show in this exercise is the solution to a problem using filters for functions other than the obvious intention.

The problem: Realistic reflections cast on a large body of water. If the need for reflections in a pool were needed then the solution is simple. Paste a copy of the objects being reflected into the pool, flip them vertically and then apply a Ripple filter to the pool. That is the obvious. But if the objects being reflected are far away as in the image shown above, the Ripple filter will give the impression that there are tidal waves along the shoreline.

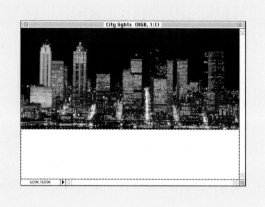

1. To follow along, use the image of any city skyline or country setting in which all the elements are in the distance. The canvas size should be enlarged to accommodate the reflection area.

Creating the first alpha channel

2. With the Rectangle Marquee selection tool, select the bottom portion of the image. Press Command-I to invert it to black.

3. Go up to the Select menu and choose Save Selection.

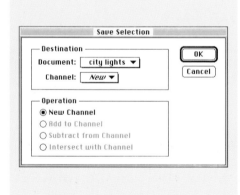

4. In the dialog box that appears, the Document should be the current document you are working in. The Channel should be New. This will create the first of your alpha channels where the masks for all the effects will be created.

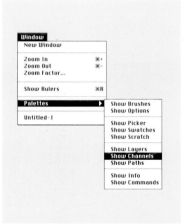

5. Go up to the Windows menu and under Palettes, choose Show Channels.

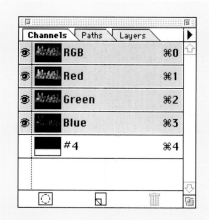

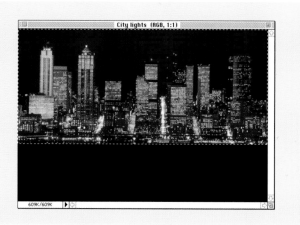

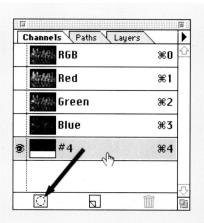

6. The alpha channel you just created should be visible in the Channels window. If you are working in RGB, it will be called #4. If you are working in CMYK, it will be called #5.

Creating the reflection

7. Return to the color channel (RGB or CMYK) by clicking once on the RGB panel in the Channels window. With the Rectangle Marquee selection tool, select the top portion of the image. Press Command-C to copy it into the clipboard.

8. Go to the Channels window and place the cursor over the alpha channel (#4) and click and drag it over the little icon of a box with a circle at the lower left of the Channels window. This will load the alpha channel as a selection over the RGB image.

9. Go to the Edit menu and choose Paste Into. The skyline will fall into place in the water. DO NOT DESELECT.

10. Go to the Image menu and choose Flip Vertical. The image will now be upside down. Move it into position directly under the skyline above.

Adjusting opacity

11. It will add to the realism if the reflection is not as strong as the actual scene. To accomplish this, you will bring down the opacity slightly. ● *Pressing the number keys on the keyboard will change the opacity. 5 will be 50%, etc.*

Creating the effect of water

None of the actual water filters (Ripple, Waves, ZigZag) will work here. These filters give you very realistic liquid effects. The problem here is that these effects are for liquids close to your field of vision. In the case of the image being created here, these filters would give the appearance of tidal waves along the shore. If you look at an actual scene, you will notice that the reflection seems to streak away from the source. The Motion Blur filter will give you that effect. Even though that is not what the name infers, the end result is what you need.

12. Go to the Filters menu down to the Blur sub menu and choose Motion Blur.

13. In the dialog box you will find a box where you can preview the effect. Placing the cursor within the box allows you to scroll around the image to find the best area to show the effect. Just below the box are two controls to let you zoom in or out for a better view. The Preview button on the right will preview the actual image. Note: this takes longer for the screen to redraw itself each time.

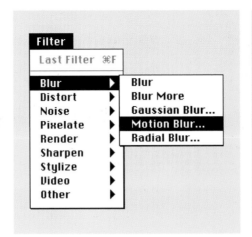

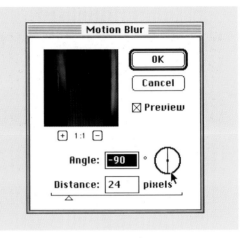

At the bottom, the angle entry box lets you input a direction for the blur or you can do it visually with the small wheel to the right of it.

The bar at the bottom lets you enter the distance. For the reflection, straight up and down or -90° is needed. We chose 24 for the distance, you can choose whatever looks good to you.

The result is a realistic reflection of the city in the water.

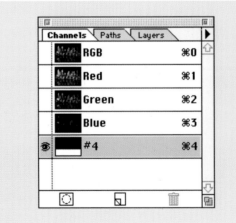

Creating ripples in the water

14. To give motion to the water, it is necessary to create ripples. Again, the ripple filter will not work here. In the Channels window, click on channel #4 to bring you to that channel.

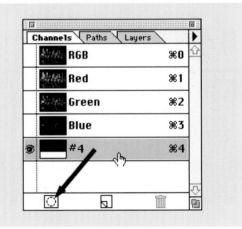

15. Load the channel onto itself by dragging it over the small Load Selection icon at the bottom of the window. This will make it a selection within the alpha channel itself.

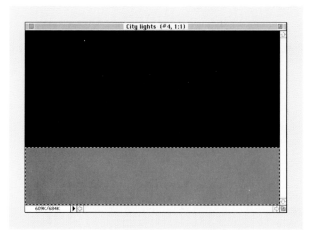

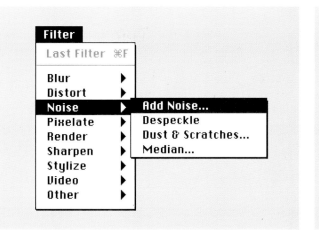

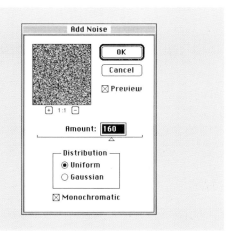

16. Since you are currently in an alpha channel, the Swatches window will display only gray tones. Choose a medium gray tone.

Press Option-Delete to fill the selected area with the gray.

17. Go to the Filter menu and under the Noise sub menu, choose Add Noise...

18. In the dialog box that pops up enter 160 for the amount and click OK.

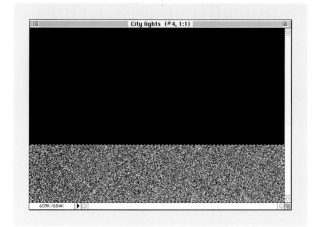

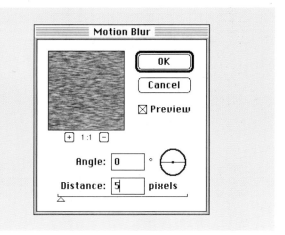

The result will look like the above. DO NOT DESELECT.

19. Go to the Filter menu and choose the Motion Blur filter again.

20. This time the direction is horizontal and the distance is 5.

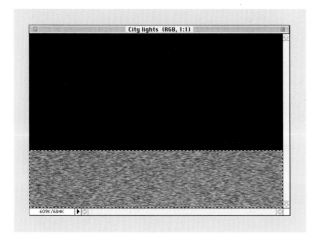

The result of the Motion Blur filter on the noise should look like above.

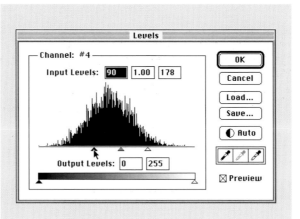

21. Contrast is needed between the waves. Under the Image menu, go to the Adjust sub menu and choose Levels. In the Dialog box which pops up, move the triangles under the histogram toward the center as shown here. Moving these sliders will change the value of the grays within the area of the histogram.

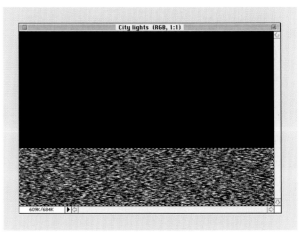

The result should look like the above. Return to the RGB channel by clicking RGB in the Channels window.

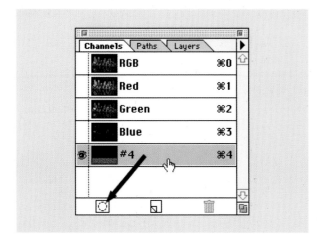

22. Load the alpha channel by dragging it over the Load Selection icon in the Channels window. ☀ *Press Command-H to hide the marching ants of the selection.*

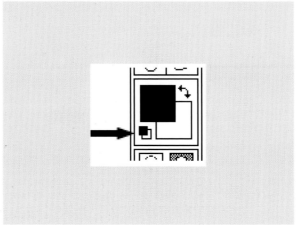

23. Reset the foreground and background colors to black and white by clicking on the small icon in the colors section of the toolbox.

24. Press Option-Delete to fill the selected area with black. This gives the appearance of waves in the water. DO NOT DESELECT.

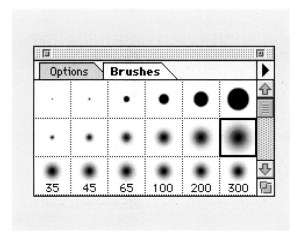

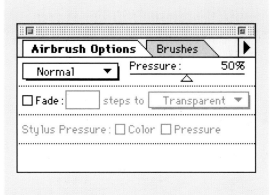

25. Choose the Airbrush tool. In the Brush Size window choose the size shown above.

26. In the Brush Options window, choose 50% for the pressure.

27. Choose white for the foreground color, and with the Airbrush, spray small patches of white along the shore to simulate reflections of the bright lights in the water.

The end result should look like this.

8

Lens Flare

Photoshop began its life as a darkroom inside a computer. From simple cropping to dodging and burning, many Photoshop features simulate professional photographic effects.

We start with a simple image.

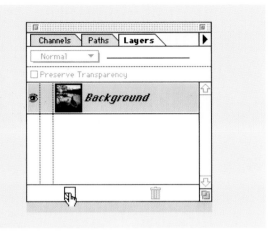

1. Create a new layer by clicking the New Layer icon in the Layers palette.

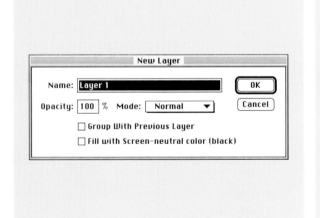

2. The New Layer dialog box appears. ⬛ *Hold down the Option key to create a new layer without opening the New Layer dialog box.*

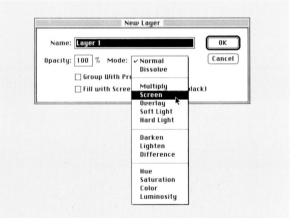

3. Select Screen from the Mode pop-up menu. ⬛ *Screen mode looks at the color information in each channel and multiplies the inverse of the blend and base colors. The result is always a lighter color. Screening with black leaves the color unchanged. Screening with white produces white. The effect is similar to painting over an area with bleach.*

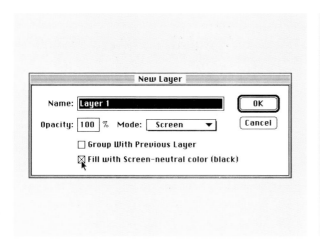

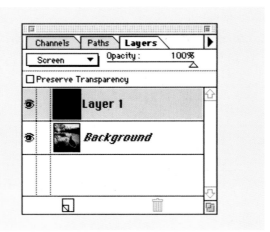

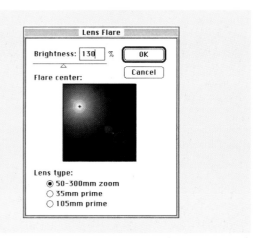

4. Fill the new layer with black (the screen-neutral color). *Filling with a screen-neutral color ensures that the background of the new, screened layer is neutral—that is, transparent.*

5. The new layer appears above the background layer. Make sure that the black layer is selected for the next step.

6. Run the Lens Flare filter on the black layer only. In this example we used a brightness of 130%. *The Lens Flare filter can be used only in RGB mode. It does not work in CMYK mode.*

7. Voila! A beautiful lens flare. Use the Move tool to drag the flare anywhere on the image. If desired, adjust the layers opacity for different effects. *By applying filters to layer's, you can make unlimited changes without affecting the underlying image.*

9

Lighting Effects Filter

One of the new filters included with version 3.0 is the Lighting Effects filter. With it, the lighting of an image can be changed to match another image into which it is being composited. Another use is to completely alter the mood of an image.

The image shown above has been dramatically altered from its original form with the use of this filter plus a few alpha channel and Path tool tricks.

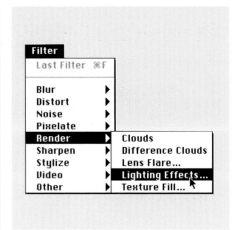

Above is the image in its original form.

1. The Lighting Effects filter is chosen from the Filters menu.

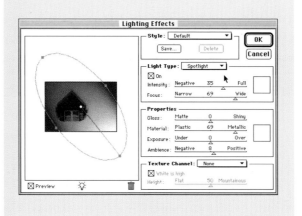

The Lighting Effects filter's dialog box offers a wide variety of controls. The left side of the box provides a work and preview area. Multiple light sources can be added by dragging the small Lightbulb icon from below the box and placing it where you want the light to originate from. Likewise, lights can be deleted by dragging them into the Trash icon at the bottom. Style has a variety of preset lighting conditions. New sets can be saved into this menu or deleted.

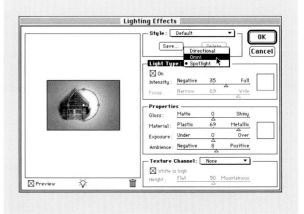

2. Light Type gives you three choices. Omni is chosen, which centers the light source, since the effect is the light emanating from the window.

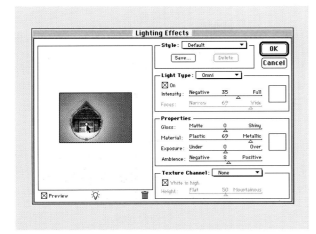

3. The center of the light is moved to be centered within the window frame.

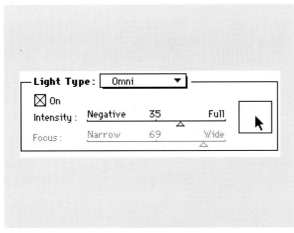

Selecting the color for the light
4. Clicking on the box at the far right of the Light Type section of the dialog box allows you to select the color of the light source.

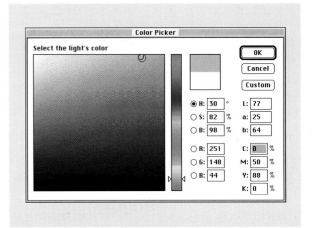

The Color Picker pops up and a bright yellow/orange is selected.

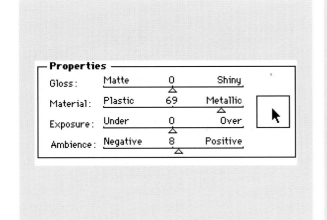
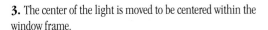

Choosing the falloff color
5. The same box in the Properties section allows you to choose the color the light will fade off to.

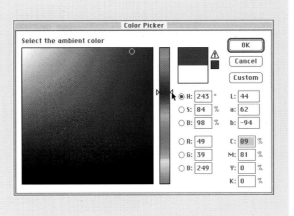

This time a dark blue is selected.

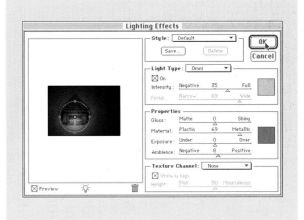

The result can be viewed in the preview portion of the dialog box. Click OK to apply the effect.

The result. The mood has changed from a day scene to a night scene.

Turning on the lights

6. With the Rectangle selection tool, select the window panes.

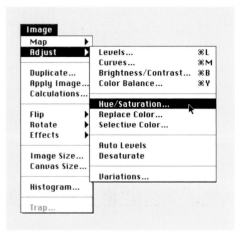

7. Under the Image menu, go to the Adjust sub menu and choose Hue/Saturation.

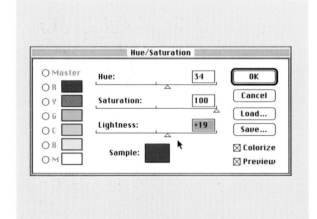

Activate the Colorize option on the lower right of the dialog box. This will totally change the color (hue) of the selected area without affecting the luminosity. Move the Hue slider at the top to the right into the yellow range. Move the Lightness slider at the bottom to lighten the area.

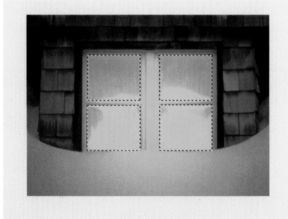

The result is the look of the lights being turned on inside the house.

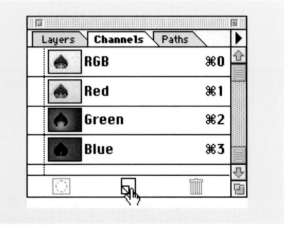

Creating an alpha channel

8. Holding down the Option key, click on the Document icon in the Channels window. This will create a new, blank alpha channel.

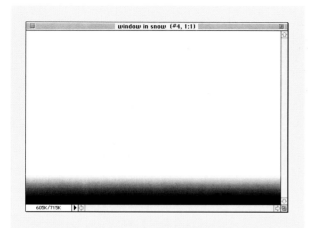

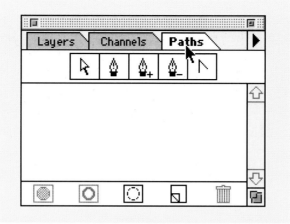

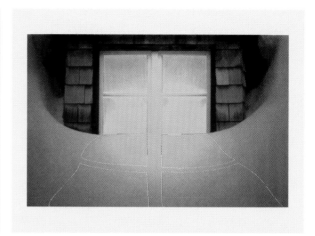

9. With the Gradient tool, create a gradient from black to white in the same position as the one shown above. This channel will be used as the basis for the reflection of the light onto the snow in front of the window. The gradient will produce the effect of the reflection gradually fading as it gets further away.

Creating a path for the reflection
10. Choose the Path tool. It is found as one of the tabs in the Channels/Layers/Paths window.

Create a set of paths which closely resemble the ones shown above.

Save the path by dragging the Working Path shown in the Paths window down to the Document icon at the bottom of the window.

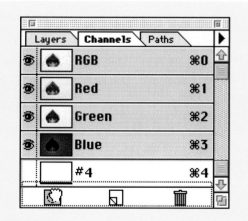

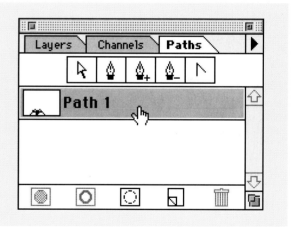

11. Load the alpha channel as a selection by going to the Channels window and dragging it over the Make Selection icon at the bottom of the window.

The marching ants will appear and display the selection from the 50% gray to the white of the alpha channel.

12. In the Paths window, click once on the Path previously saved to bring it up on the image.

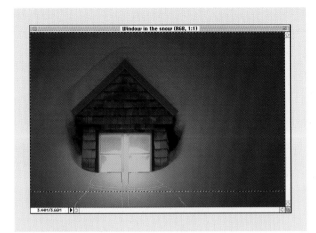

The path will appear over the image and the marching ants of the current selection.

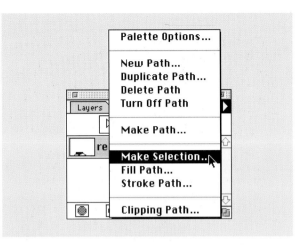

Making a selection from a path

13. On the upper right corner of the Path window is a small arrow. Clicking on it will drop down a menu with options for the paths. Choose Make Selection.

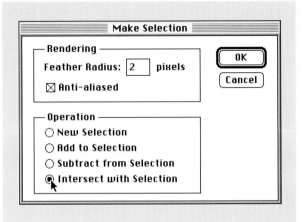

In the dialog box which appears, a Feather of 2 is entered to soften the edges. Since a selection is currently active, the Operations box is fully available. Intersect with Selection is chosen. To further understand what is happening here refer to the section on alpha channels on page 38.

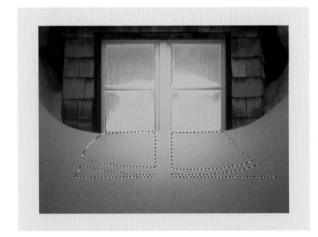

The result is a selected area like the one shown above.

Choosing the reflection color

14. Using the Color Picker tool (eyedropper), a bright yellow is chosen from the light areas within the window.

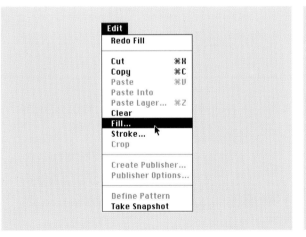

15. Choose Fill from the Edit menu.

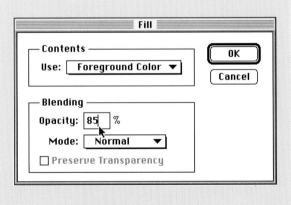

16. The Foreground color with an Opacity of 85% is chosen.

The end result is a new image completely different in mood from the original.

10

Alpha Channels

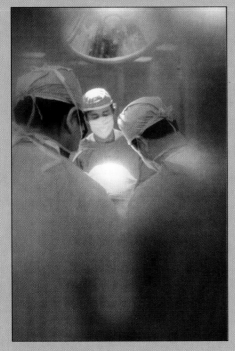

Alpha channels are one of the most powerful features of Photoshop. They are also the most misunderstood of the functions. Alpha channels are 8-bit layers used for masking images. To better grasp the concept of an alpha channel it is necessary to understand the concept of a mask.

A mask is essentially a stencil, like a cardboard with a cut out area used to paint uniform letters or pictures onto a surface.

With traditional medium, an image like the one shown above, is to be modified in the specific area of the leaves behind the mushroom.

A mask is created by placing a sheet of frisket or vellum (transparent material papers) over the art.

The area to be modified is cut out with a knife.

The cut out area is exposed while the remaining frisket protects the covered artwork from change. Paint, pencil or any other media can be applied to the art in the cut out areas.

Upon finishing the modification, the mask is removed and the modified art is viewed.

An alpha channel is basically the same concept. 100% black represents the mask and 100% white equals the cutout.

When an alpha channel is applied to an image, wherever the alpha channel is black, the image is protected. Where the channel is white, the image will be modified. Any modification which can be applied to an image in Photoshop, can be applied through an alpha channel. This includes all the Adjust controls, Filters and Paste commands.

To create an alpha channel of a specific area or shape, simply select the area and choose Save Selection from the Image menu. If you want to create a new channel for the entire image then all you have to do is click on the Document icon at the bottom of the Channels palette.

All of the alpha channels are stored with the image as long as it is in Photoshop format. Other formats will allow you to keep one or two of the alpha channels. Keep in mind that these channels are used as masks and have no bearing on the image itself.

In programs such as Adobe Premiere, the Alpha channel can be used as a mask through which other sources of video can be seen. The one important difference between a traditional mask and an alpha channel is the fact that an alpha channel is an 8-bit mask. This means it has 256 levels of gray which can be applied to it. These gray levels determine the opacity of the channel. Unlike traditional masks which totally expose an area, the alpha channel can make that exposure a gradual one. The level of gray determines the exposure level. For example, a 50% gray will expose the image to a 50% modification.

A good example of this effect is an old photographic technique of blurring out the outer edges of an image by applying petroleum jelly to the outer edges of the lens. This same effect can be achieved by creating a radial gradient in an alpha channel which has black at the center with a gradient to white at the outer edges.

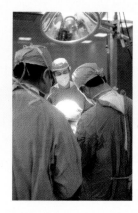

Start with an image to be modified. By clicking on the Document icon in the Channels palette, an alpha channel is created.

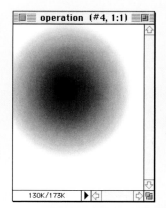

In the alpha channel, using the Blend tool in Radial mode, a blend is created that contains a radial gradient from black to white.

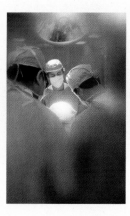

When the alpha channel is loaded onto the image, a Gaussian Blur filter, from the Filters menu, is applied which will give the same result as in the traditional method.

An alpha channel is stored with the file and can be reused as many times as needed. This is essential when you consider the possibility of the client making changes. This is another difference from the traditional mask which would require a new frisket every time the same area was to be modified.

Any Photoshop 3.0 file can have up to 24 channels resident within the file. If the image is an RGB file, the Red, Green and Blue occupy 3 channels which frees up 21 channels to be alpha channels. If an image is CMYK, then the Cyan, Magenta, Yellow and Black take up 4 channels with the remaining 20 to be assigned as alpha channels.

The creation of an alpha channel enlarges the size (storage) of a file. This is because you are adding another 8-bit channel to the existing 8-bit channels that make up the color information. Also, you might want to have more channels than the 24 provided. This is why when you choose the Save Selection from the menu method to create the channel you are given the option to save it to a new file. By putting the alpha channels somewhere else, the color file retains its original size and the new file can store all 24 channels as alpha channels.

This feature is also handy if you are creating alpha channels for a file of a format other than Photoshop. It is important to note that some formats do not store the alpha channels (see the section on formats). With this option, you can have all your alpha channels in their own file and virtually have thousands of them.

There are two ways of creating an alpha channel. When an area is selected in an image, going to the Select menu and choosing the Save Selection will create an alpha channel for the selected area.

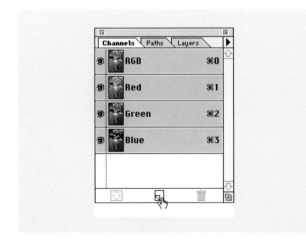

🍎 *If you wish to create a new alpha channel without a selection, Option-clicking on the Document icon at the bottom of the Channels window will create a new channel.*

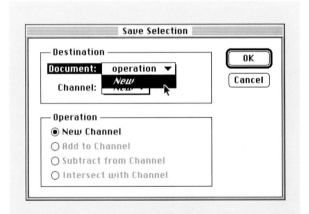

If the Save Selection method is used, a dialog box will appear which offers options for the alpha channel being created. Here, a new or existing document can be selected as the destination for the channel.

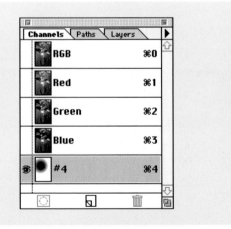

The new channel will appear in the Channels window. Clicking on it will bring you to that channel. The channel currently highlighted is the one being written to. Additional channels can be viewed by selecting the Eye icon to the left of each channel.

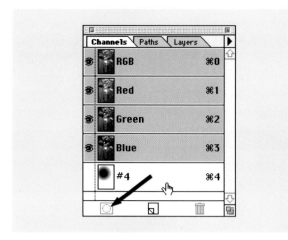

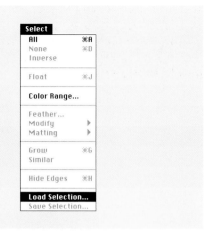

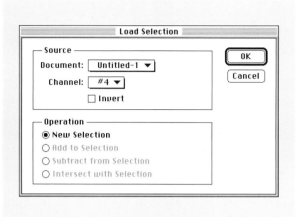

There are three methods to load the channel (make the mask active). The first is to click and drag the channel in the Channels palette over the Make Selection icon at the bottom of the Channels palette.

The second method is to choose Load Selection from the Select menu. The third is to simply click on the desired channel in the Channels palette with the Option button pressed.

If Load Selection is used, a dialog box will appear which provides options for the way the selection will be applied. First, it lets you determine from where the channel will be read and where it will be applied.

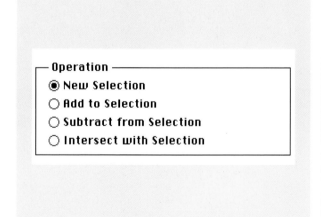

The Operation section of the dialog box determines how the selection will interact with other selections which might currently be active. If nothing is selected, New Selection will be the only choice.

If something is selected, this will override it and create a new selected area. The area shown above was selected before the channel was loaded.

New Selection overrode the selected area leaving a new selected area.

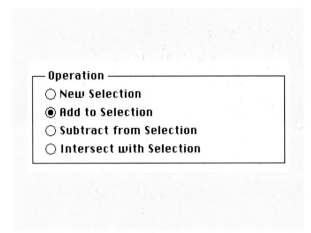

If an area is currently selected, Add to Selection will add the contents of the alpha channels selection to the current selected area.

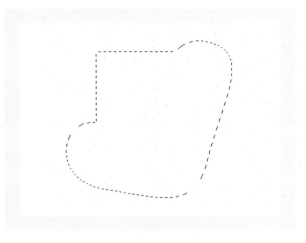

Using the examples, the result would look like this.

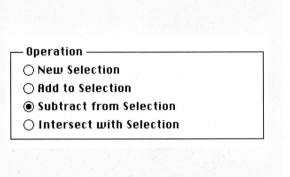

If an area is currently selected, Subtract from Selection will subtract the contents of the alpha channels selection to the current selected area.

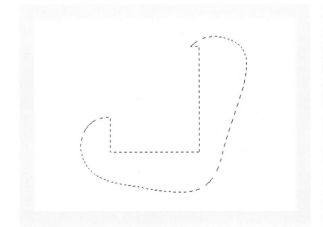

The subtracted area.

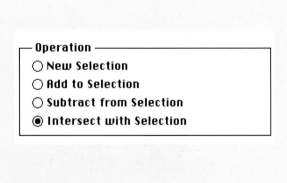

If an area is currently selected, Intersect with Selection will select only the area where the two selections intersect each other.

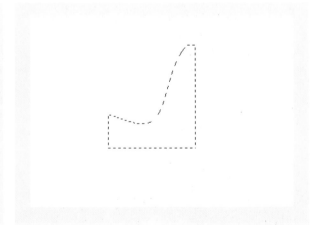

The selection is the intersection of the rectangle and the previous shaped selection.

11

Rings on a Planet

Celestial scenes are appearing everywhere nowadays, from ads or articles on telecommunications to a variety of science fiction materials showing up in games.

Planets can easily be created using various filter effects for the surface texture. If you want to add rings to the planet, the process is very simple.

To follow this exercise, create or scan two files—one of a starry sky and one of a planet. For the purposes of this step-by-step tutorial, all measurements are based on images which are 640 by 480, at a resolution of 72 pixels.

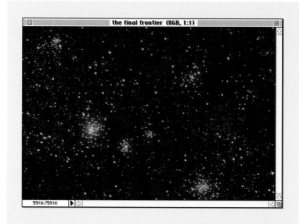

1. A starry sky is opened to serve as our background.

2. A planet is created and selected and copied to the clipboard.

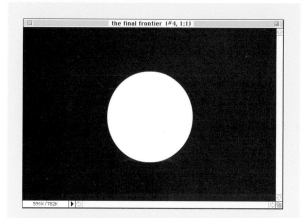

Giving the planet depth

The planet is pasted into the sky and an alpha channel is immediately created with the Save Selection command under the Select menu. For effect, a dark side will be created for the planet.

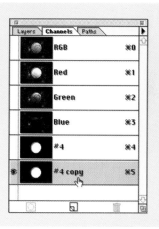

3. A copy of the alpha channel is made by dragging the channel over the new channel Document icon at the bottom of the Channels window.

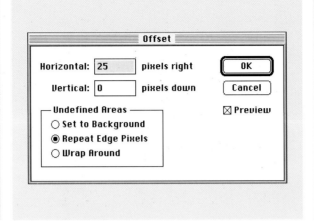

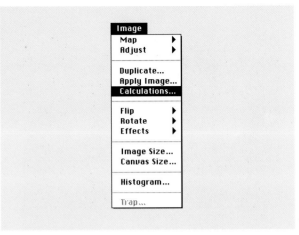

4. A Gaussian Blur filter is applied with a radius of 20.

5. An Offset filter is applied 25 pixels to the right and 0 for down. Repeat Edge Pixels is selected to retain the black on the outside edge of the channel.

6. Under the Image menu, Calculations is chosen.

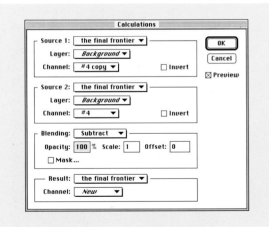

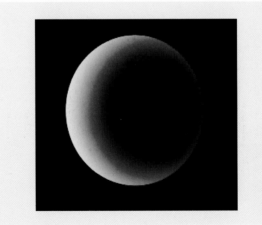

7. In the dialog box that appears, Source 1 is the current file. Layer is Background. The copy of the alpha channel is the Channel. Source 2 is the current file. Layer is Background. The original alpha channel is the Channel. The Blending is set to Subtract. Opacity is 100%, Scale is set to 1 and Offset is set to 0. The Result should be the current file with New for the channel.

The resulting channel should look like the image above.

8. Back in the RGB channel, the alpha channel is made a selection. The selection is filled with 100% black. This casts a shadow effect for the dark side of the planet.

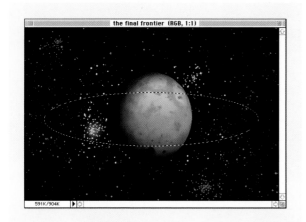

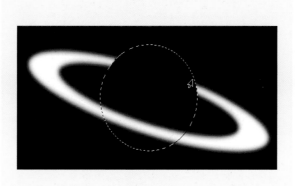

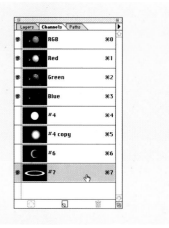

Creating the rings

9. With the Elliptical selection tool with a Feather set to 4, select an oval similar to the one shown above. If the position is not quite right you can either reselect it or move the marching ants by holding down the Option and Command keys while dragging the selection into position.

10. With the same tool but with the Command key pressed to subtract from the selection, drag another oval to cut out the center. Start from a position inside from the top and side as shown above. ● *Holding down the Option and Command keys while dragging a selection allows you to move the marching ants (selection marquee) of the selection without moving the contents of the selection.*

11. The rings are then saved to an alpha channel.

12. It is necessary to rotate the rings. In the Channels window, the rings channel is selected to write to. The Eye icon in the RGB channels are turned on in order to view them.

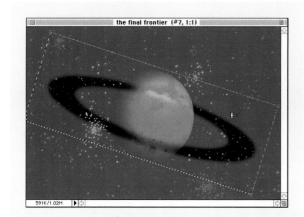

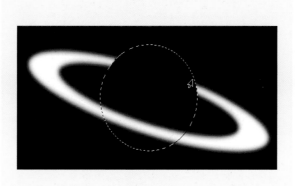

13. Using the Rectangular selection tool, the rings are selected.

Black is chosen for the background color. This will ensure that no holes are created when the rings are rotated. Free is chosen from the Rotate sub menu of the Image menu. The rings are rotated to the angle shown above.

14. Go to the alpha channel of the ring by clicking on it in the Channels window. Turn off the Eye icons for the RGB so the ring channel is the only one visible.

15. Load the first alpha channel of the planet as a selection onto the ring channel by dragging it over the Load Selection icon at the bottom of the window. With a Black Paint Brush, paint out the portion of the rings which fall behind the planet.

16. Back in the RGB channel, the rings alpha channel is loaded.

17. A color for the rings is selected and then using the Fill command under the Edit menu, the color is applied. The opacity is brought down to 20% to allow the stars to show through the rings.

12

Cut-out Effect

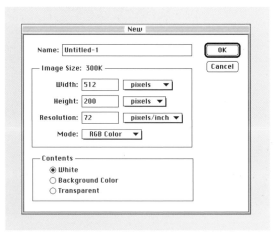

The effect of a cut out is easily achieved in Photoshop. This is the illusion that a shape (text, etc.) has been cut out of an image exposing another image underneath.

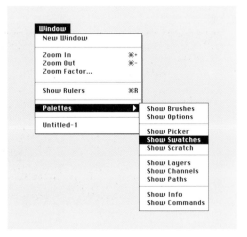

Starting a new file
1. Click on New in the File menu.

In the box that pops up, enter 512 for the width and 200 for the height.

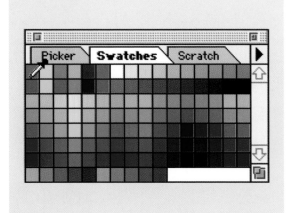

Choosing color
2. If your Colors palette is not on the screen, bring it up by selecting Show Swatches from the Palettes sub menu of the Windows menu. Choose the bright red on the upper left.

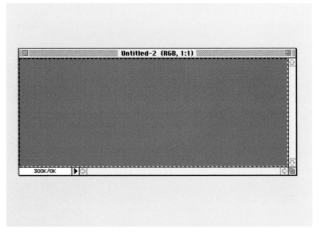

3. Press Command-A to select all. Press Option-Delete to fill the area with 100% of the foreground color which is red.

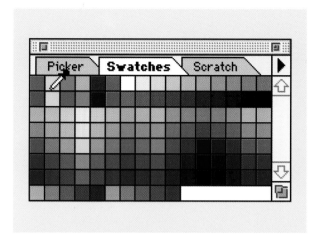

4. Choose the bright yellow to the right of the red in the Color palette.

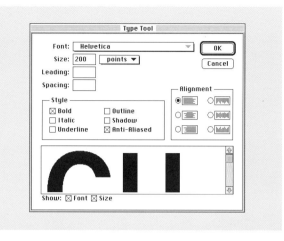

Creating type

5. Select the Type tool, click in the window to create some type. Type the word Cut. Use the Bold and Anti-Aliased option and enter 200 for the size in the text dialog box as in the figure shown here. Click OK.

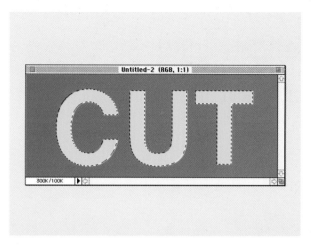

The type comes in selected (DO NOT DESELECT).

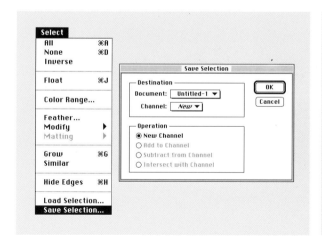

Saving a selection

6. With the word still selected, choose the Save Selection command under the Select menu.

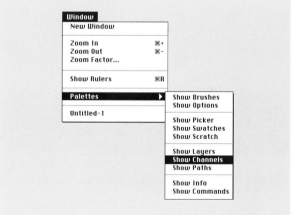

7. Choose the Show Channels command under the Windows menu.

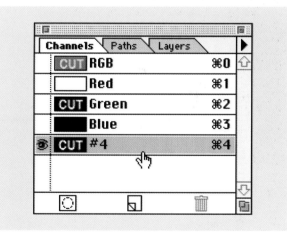

8. In the Channels window, click on #4 to bring you to that channel.

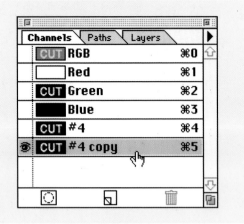

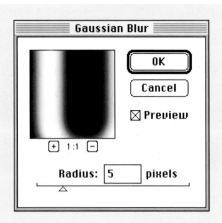

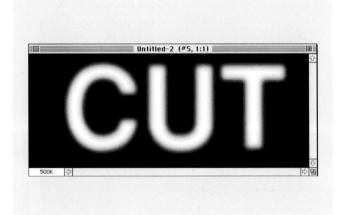

9. Drag it over the Document icon at the bottom of the window to make a duplicate of it. The duplicate will be titled #4 Copy.

10. Choose the filter Gaussian Blur from the Blur choice of the Filters menu. Enter 5 for the value and click OK.

The result is blurred type.

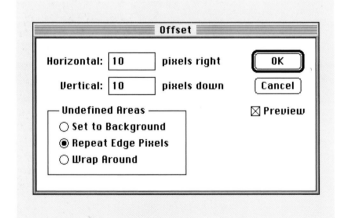

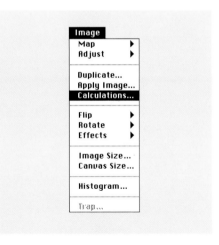

11. Go to the Other choice under the Filters menu and select Offset. In the dialog box that pops up, enter 10 in each box and click Repeat Edge Pixels.

The result is that the contents of the channel are shifted to the lower right.

12. Go to the Calculations choice under the Image menu.

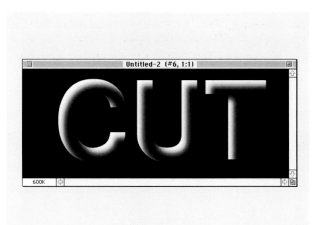

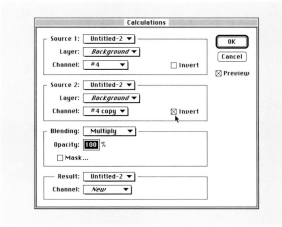

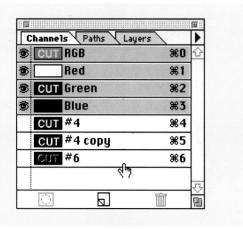

13. In the dialog box that appears, for Source 1, the channel is set to #4. Source 2, the channel is set to #4 copy with the Invert choice selected. Blending is set to Multiply. Destination is the same file with channel to New.

The result exposes the inside left edge of the type.

14. Press Command-0 (zero) to return to the RGB channel or click on the RGB panel in the Channels window. Load #6 by dragging it over the Make Selection icon in the Channels window.

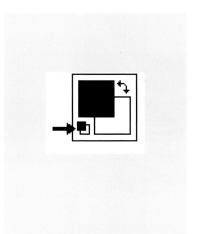

16. Press Option-Delete to fill the selected area with black. If not dark enough, press Option-Delete again. You're done!

15. Return your colors to black and white by clicking the small icon in the Tools palette.

13

Creating a Grid

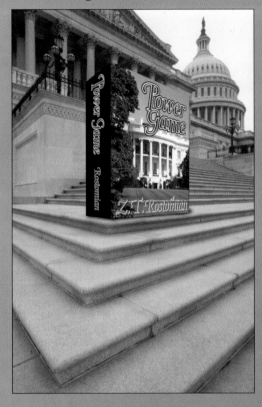

There are many people out there that have requested grid capabilities in Photoshop. That feature has always been there. It just requires a little creative manipulation. Albeit, there is no Snap to Grid feature, but grids which can serve as guides are possible.

The task of creating these grids can be done in either layers or alpha channels. Here we will show the alpha channel solution which will also demonstrate some of the other functions of alpha channels.

We are going to place a book on the steps shown above. The problem is the exaggerated angle of the image. It is vital to follow that perspective to make it seem as if the book is really there. Just as in traditional illustration techniques, perspective guide lines from a vanishing point will be needed. The vanishing point is the point at which all lines converge. In this image they extend beyond the boundaries. A larger canvas area is needed to accommodate these vanishing points.

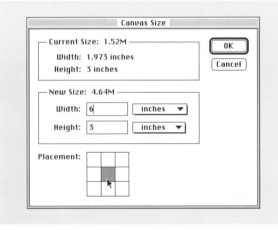

2. In the Canvas Size dialog box, the new width dimension is entered. The checkerboard at the bottom lets you position the current image within the new canvas. We chose centered.

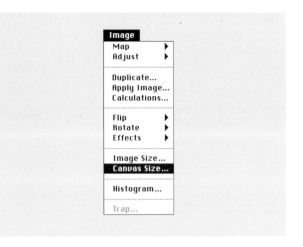

Creating a larger canvas

1. Canvas Size is summoned from the Image menu.

The new enlarged canvas appears.

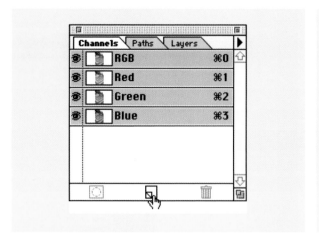

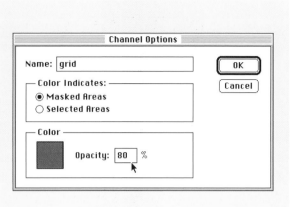

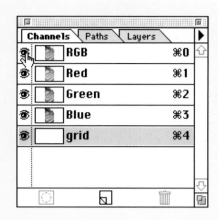

Creating a new alpha channel

3. In the Channels palette, a new channel is created by clicking on the Document icon at the bottom of the palette.

4. The channel is named "Grid." Color Indicates is set to Masked Areas. Clicking in the colored box allows you to change the color in which the channel will be viewed when viewed over the RGB channel. A bright red is chosen because it will contrast with the RGB. The opacity is increased to 80% for better viewing.

5. The new channel comes in completely black. Press Command-I to invert it to white.

6. In the Channels palette, click the Eye icon in the RGB channel. Be sure that the alpha channel is the one being written to as indicated by gray in the example above.

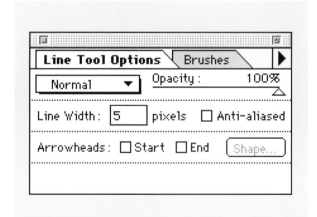

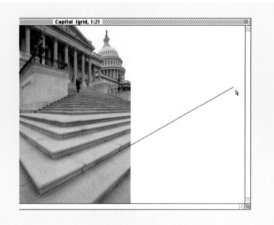

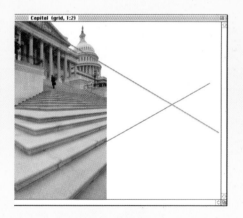

Creating the grid

7. Double-click the Line tool. In its Options palette, a line width is chosen which will be easy to see in the image.

8. A line is drawn which follows the angle of the step.

9. A second line is drawn which follows the roof line. Where the two intersect is the vanishing point for that side.

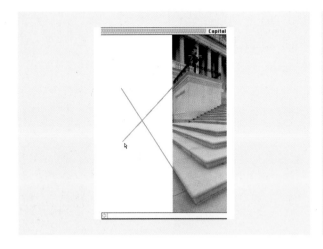

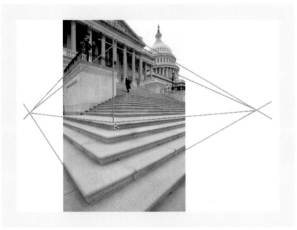

10. The same is done for the opposite side.

11. A vertical line is drawn where the corner of the spine of the book will be placed.

12. Lines are then drawn from the vanishing points to the vertical line. These are the guides for the book.

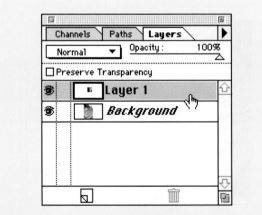

Bringing in the book image to be distorted

13. The book is now brought in by selecting it, and with the Move tool, dragged over to the Capitol image.

14. It is placed in its own Layer and made the active layer.

15. In the Channels palette, the Eye icon is turned on for the Grid channel.

16. The front cover of the book is selected with the Marquee tool.

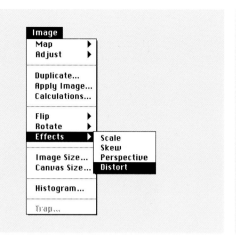
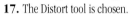

Distorting the image

17. The Distort tool is chosen.

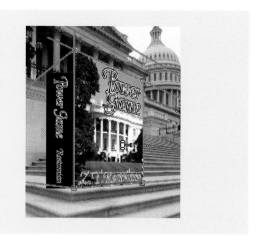

18. The cover is distorted to the shape outlined by the guides.

19. The same is done to the spine of the book. A little shadow is added beneath the book and the image is realistic.

14

Selecting Hair

There are situations when the selection tools (Lasso, Marquee, etc.) cannot be used for separating parts of an image for modification. In such cases, it is easier to use the information in the image to make the selection.

The image above was chosen to create the mood shot to the left. The one element which presented a problem was the highlights in the hair. The first thing necessary was to remove these highlights. Selecting hair is a difficult process with the selection tools.

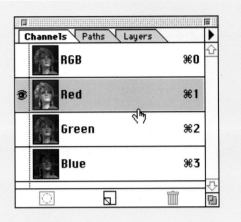

Determining the source of the problem

1. Study the information within the image by looking at the individual colors that make up the image. In the Channels palette, each color channel is selected individually by clicking on it.

What needs to be determined is which channel has the problem. Here we see the Red channel which shows the image has a large amount of red. ❤ *The lighter the tones in a channel, the more saturation of color.*

The Green channel shows relative darkness in the area of the highlights.

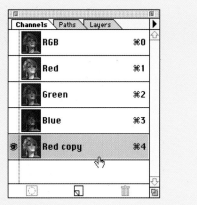

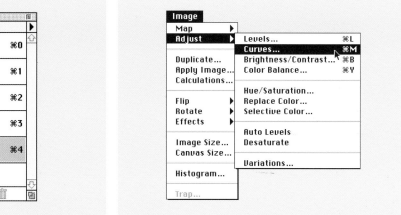

The Blue channel is the darkest of all, signifying the lack of blue in the highlight area.

Duplicating a channel

The highlights are most prominent in the Red channel. This channel will serve as the basis for a mask to isolate the highlights.

2. The Red channel is duplicated by dragging it over the Document icon at the bottom of the Channels palette.

Separating the trouble area

3. Curves is selected from the Adjust sub menu of the Image menu.

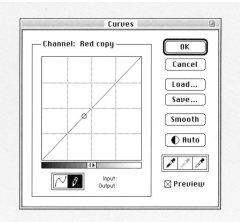

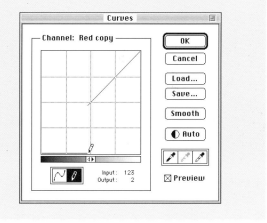

4. Passing the cursor over the image, the cursor turns into the Eyedropper cursor.

In the Curves dialog box the density level of the color over which the cursor passes is indicated by a small ball.

5. The position of the highlights is established. All the tones darker than it are converted to black by drawing a straight line along the bottom of the dialog box.

The result is all the dark tones go to black.

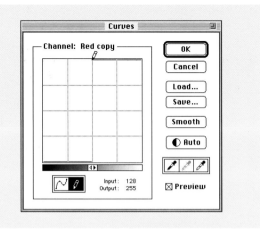

6. The highlight and all the tones above it are brought to white.

The result is a high contrast image.

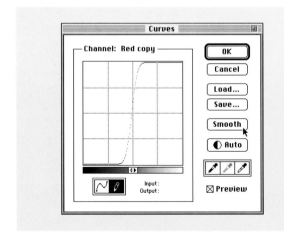

7. To soften the edges of the hair mask, the Smooth button is pressed.

This will create a ramp between the black and white. Press OK to exit the Curves dialog box.

8. With a Black Paintbrush the areas of the face and jewelry are painted over to protect them within the alpha channel. The result is a channel for the highlighted area of the hair.

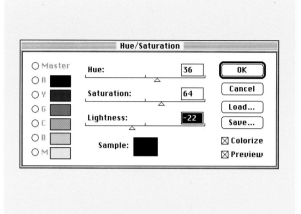

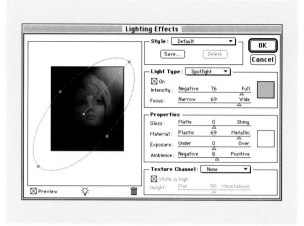

Toning down the highlights

9. When the channel is made a Selection, the hair is selected.

10. At this point the modification can be performed. In the case of this image, Hue/Saturation was used. The selected area was Colorized to match the rest of the hair. The level of Saturation was reduced and darkened.

Changing the mood

11. Finally, the Lighting Effects filter was applied.

15

Creating Templates for Illustrator

There are many occasions when it is necessary to use Photoshop to create a template for use in Adobe Illustrator. Here, we will show two situations where this is useful.

The first is the creation of art for a logotype or trademark. There are times a client provides a printed version of their logo which you must digitize. Scanning the logo into the computer is the obvious solution. The problem is that the logo is in bitmap form. Printing this file from within a page-layout program will produce "jaggies" or rough edges at the outer edges of the logo. Furthermore, if the image is enlarged, the degradation will increase.

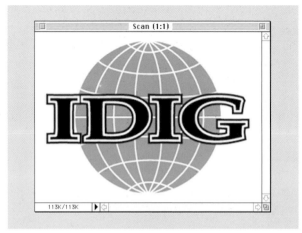

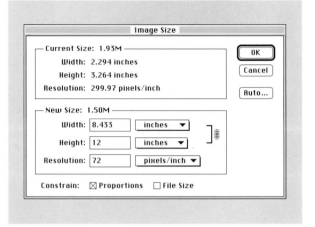

The solution is to trace the scan. There are programs which will do this automatically such as Adobe Streamline. Adobe Illustrator will take a PICT file and incorporate it into a file as a template. Using the tools in Illustrator, you trace this template. The result is an Illustrator file which will print clean regardless of size. The process for preparing the template in Photoshop is simple. First of all, when you scan the art, you should use the highest resolution possible. This will give you the most detail in the scan; otherwise, complex elements in a logo will be lost or unrecognizable from within Illustrator.

1. The scanned image is then sized to a comfortable working size. Using Image Size, found under the Image menu, the scan is sized and resampled to 72 dpi. The size is determined by the complexity. The resolution of 72 is to match the computer screen's resolution.

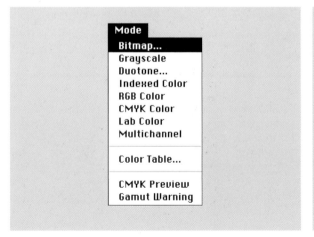

2. The mode of the image is now converted to Bitmap. Bitmap is found under the Mode menu. ⌘ *If the image is RGB, Bitmap will not be available. The image must first be converted to Grayscale.*

3. In the dialog box which appears, the top portion which deals with resolution is left as is since we already dealt with that issue in the Image Size. The option under Method will depend on the image itself. If it is a straight black and white, then 50% Threshold is fine. If there are grays in the image or you wish a softer edge, then Diffusion Dither (the default setting) is best.

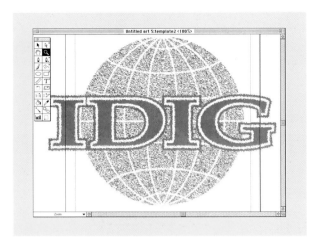

The file is then saved as a PICT file. This file is then used in Illustrator as a template to trace over.

Another use of this process is to create elements to be incorporated into a Photoshop image. Tiny or complicated details are more easily achieved in Illustrator. The image above will require railings, windows and various other details that are much better drawn in Illustrator. The basic elements were done in a 3D program.

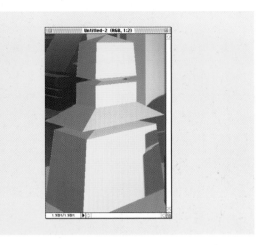

Creating a railing

1. Sections were selected and copied into new files.

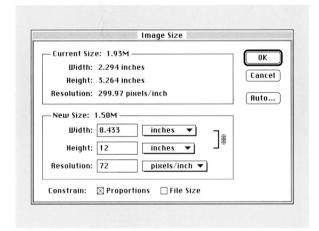

2. As in the previous example, the image is resized and resampled.

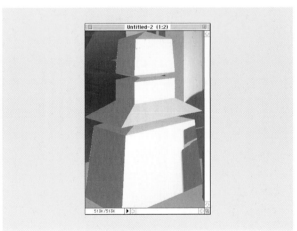

3. It is then converted to Grayscale.

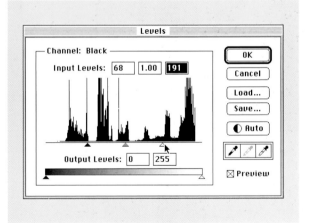

4. Using Levels, the contrast is heightened between the light and dark sides of the building.

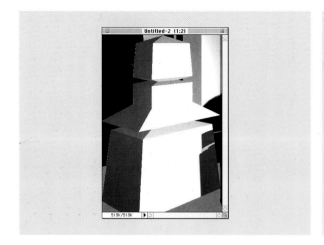

This will make it easier to distinguish them once in Illustrator.

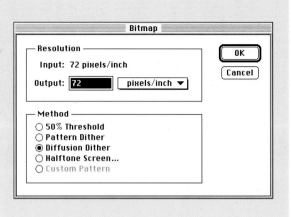

5. It is next converted into a Bitmap. Since the image has varying tones of gray, Diffusion Dither is chosen.

The result looks like the example shown above.
6. The file is then given a name and saved as a PICT file.

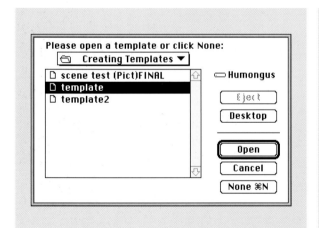

7. In Illustrator, the file which was saved to serve as the template is chosen as a template.

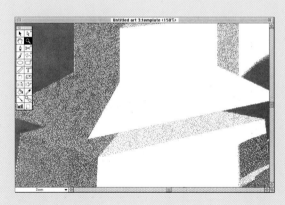

The template appears as a gray image over which you can create the necessary details.

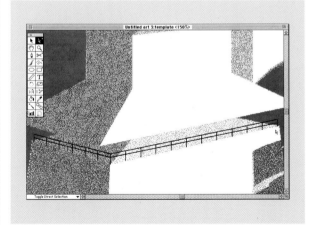

8. Using the Pen tool, a railing is created to surround the parking level in the building and saved.

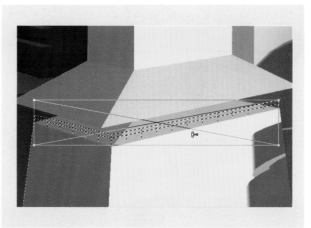

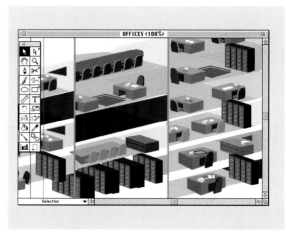

9. Back in Photoshop, the railing file is Placed.

10. The railing comes in and is sized and moved into position. The same procedure was used to create all the details visible within the windows.

Above is the Illustrator file for the offices visible through the windows of the building.

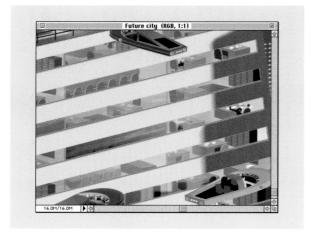

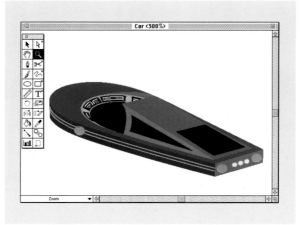

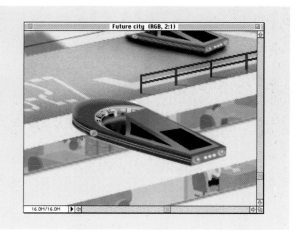

Here we see the offices placed into the Photoshop file.

Above is one of the cars in Illustrator.

The same car in the Photoshop image.

16

Patterns and Masks

The image above was created for a cover of a merchandise catalog. The various buildings in the background were created with patterns.

Patterns are usually considered as textures for wallpaper, fabrics and the like. Here we shall use them for a different effect.

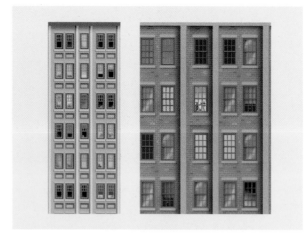

The two building facades shown above are part of the imagery that went into the cover.

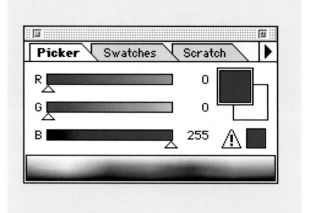

Selecting color

1. For the Foreground color a pure blue was selected which had no green or red in it.

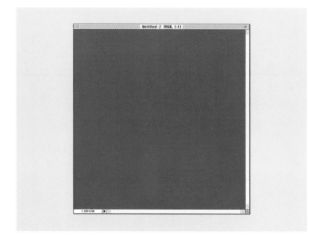

2. A new file was opened and filled with the blue.

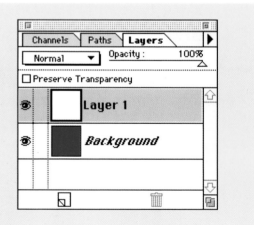

Creating a layer

3. A layer was created.

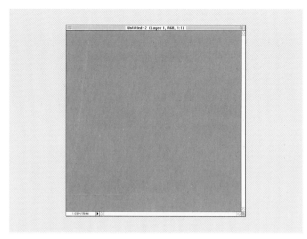

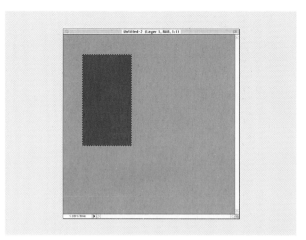

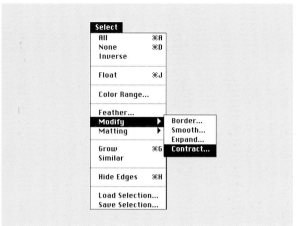

Creating a window for the pattern

4. The layer was filled with a gray which would serve as the stone material of the building.

5. An area is selected to serve as the outside boundary of the window.

6. Under the Modify sub menu of the Select menu, Contract is chosen.

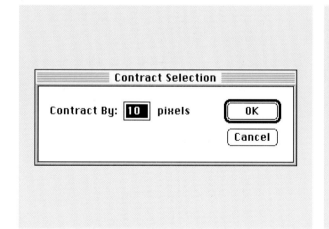

7. A value is entered to contract the selected area to form the inner panel of the window frame.

8. The selection is filled with a color.

9. The selection is contracted again and filled with another color to form the window itself.

10. Other details, such as sills, shadows and decorative items, are added in the same manner.

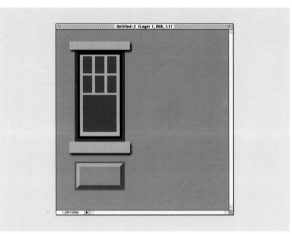

11. A new selection is made which will serve as the panes of glass. The contents of this new selection are deleted (Delete key) to expose the blue background.

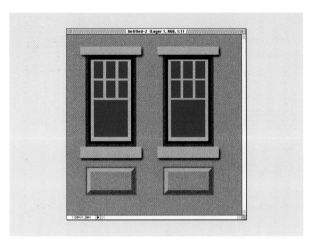

12. The entire window is copied over to the side to make two windows. The Add Noise filter is applied to the layer with the windows to simulate a stone texture.

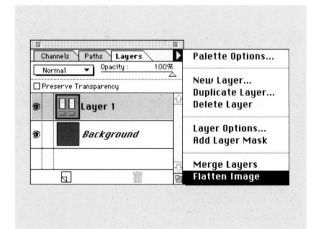

13. The two Layers are then Flattened to form one layer.

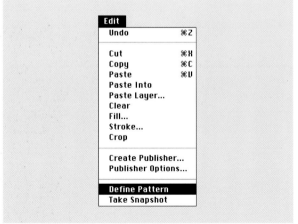

14. Command-A is pressed to select the entire image and Define Pattern is chosen from the Edit menu.

15. A New document is created which will be the building facade.

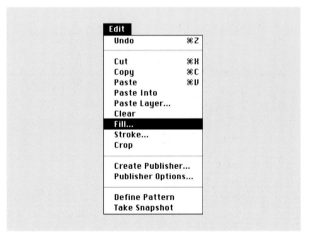

16. The Fill choice is selected from the Edit menu.

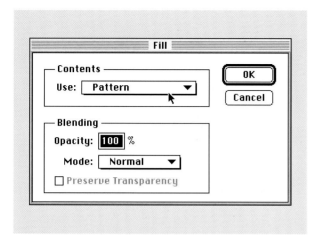

17. In the dialog box that appears, Pattern is chosen from the Contents sub menu.

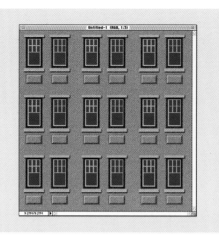

The result is a simulation of an entire building facade. To add details to the interior of the rooms, it is necessary to create a mask for the windows. This task is simple since the windows are filled with the pure blue color.

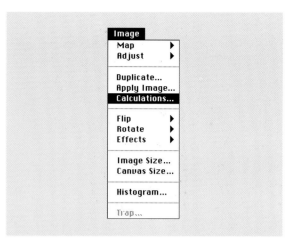

18. Calculations is chosen from the Image menu.

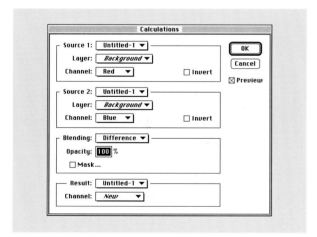

19. In the dialog box that appears, the Red channel is chosen for Source 1. The Blue channel is chosen for Source 2. Difference is chosen for the Blending method. The result is put into a new channel or a new file.

The result is an alpha channel which masks the windows for easy selection.

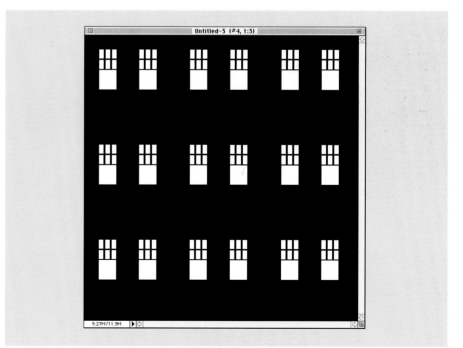

17

Edge Enhancement

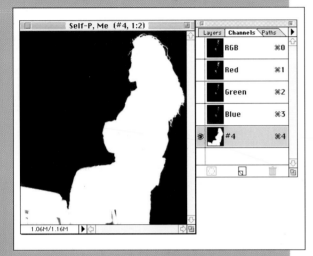

The difference between good and bad element compositing is all in the edge—big, thick, matte lines around the edges of an object are a dead giveaway of a Photoshop novice. There are a variety of tools for helping you get the best possible edge.

Edge enhancement can happen in two major ways:

• Manipulating an object's alpha channel before compositing the object into a new background.

• Enhancing the edge colors and boundaries after the selected object has been placed onto the new background (and is still a floating selection).

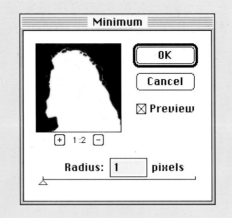

In previous versions of Photoshop, the main tools for changing the size of an object's alpha channel were the Minimum and Maximum filters (Filters>Other>Minimum, Maximum).

• Minimum: increases the size of the darker portions of an image. Also called "Choking," this process, when applied to an alpha channel or mask, shrinks the white part of the mask and enlarges the dark background of the mask. When made into a selection, or used as a mask with the Composite calculate command, this "choked" mask has the effect of making the edges of an object contract inward, decreasing the width of matte lines.

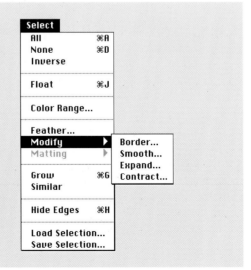

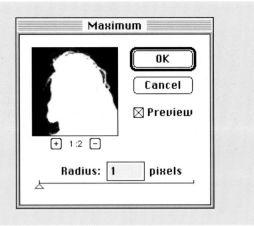

• Maximum: increases the size of the lighter portions of an image. Also called "Spreading," this process, when applied to an alpha channel or mask, expands the white part of the mask and shrinks the dark background of the mask. When made into a selection, or used as a mask with the Composite Calculate command, this "spread" mask has the effect of making the edges of an object expand outward, revealing more of the edges of the object (and less of the background).

Both of these filters have a definable parameter, expressed as pixels, though we've found that the amount of choking or spreading seems to move in larger increments than a pixel. It's also important to remember that as you work with documents of increasing resolution, the value specified for the Maximum and Minimum filters must also be increased to achieve comparable results (this holds true for any filter or effect which is expressed in pixels).

A new addition to Photoshop 3.0 adds a whole new set of options to choking and spreading masks, and in many cases, delivers much better results than using the Minimum and Maximum filters. When an object is selected, you can choose to Expand or Contract (Select>Modify>Expand, Contract) the selection, which effectively spreads and chokes the selection without having to create an alpha channel. Of course, the only way to actually see the results of an Expand or Contract (besides copying the object and pasting it into a new background) is to save the newly modified selection into an alpha channel.

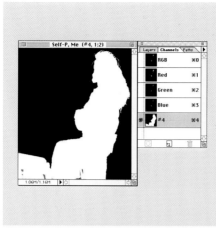

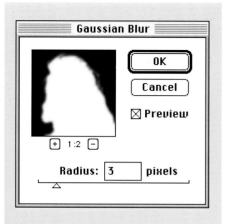

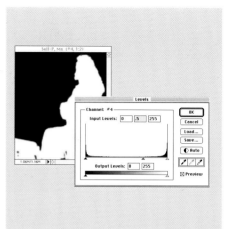

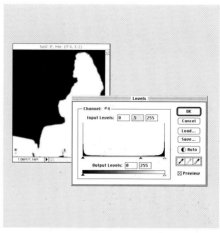

Another technique is using a combination of blurring and the Levels controls (Image>Adjust>Levels) to interactively change the choking or spreading of the edges of a mask.

1. Make your mask channel active.

2. Apply a Gaussian Blur between 1.5 and 3.5.

3. Open the Levels controls, and try moving the midpoint of the input (the gray triangular control) to the left. This has the effect of spreading the white core of the mask.

Moving the midpoint control to the right chokes the white core. The whole process is quite interactive, allowing you to dial in the exact amount of spreading or choking desired.

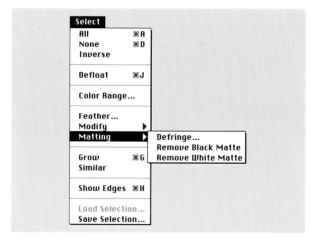

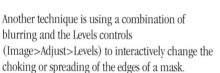

Defringing

Once an object has been selected, copied and pasted into a new background or document, there are three options for helping remove the telltale matte line (which is the result of a mask or selection which isn't quite tight enough). These options are found in the Selection>Matting sub menu. All three require that an object just be pasted into a document, or made floating by selecting Select>Float (or Command-J). The Defringe command (Selection>Matting>Defringe) is uniquely useful in removing a variety of matte lines (especially those with varying color values along the edge). The command works by taking an input value (expressed in pixels) and coming in on a tangent from every point of the selection toward the center of the floating object. It then takes the color values found inside the object and stretches the color to the edges of the selection, effectively covering the matte line with an opaque wash of color from the interior of the object.

Another neat tip is knowing to use the Border command (Select>Modify>Border) in conjunction with blurring, in order to reestablish good antialiasing on the edges of a defringed object. Now, before you go nuts with Defringing, realize one thing: if you find yourself typing double-digit values into the Defringe dialog (or three digit values, in the case of very high resolution images), then you're going to get a better result by going back and editing the actual mask used to select the object in the first place.

If you've selected objects from either pure white or black backgrounds, and plan on pasting them into colored backgrounds, you'll be interested in two new companion commands to Defringe:

Remove Black Matte: used to automatically defringe objects selected and copied from a black, or very dark background.

Remove White Matte: used to automatically defringe objects selected and copied from a white, or very light background.

In practive, we've found these latter two options a bit less useful for objects with defined black and white borders; these options seem to be made to work with objects which have pixels on the edges which are increasing in brightness or darkness.

18

Working with Layers

One of the most powerful and long-awaited features of Photoshop 3.0 is Layers. Layers allow you to combine separate bitmapped elements into a single composition, while retaining the discrete identity of each bitmapped object. Layers also deliver a way to retain many variations of an active image. This is dangerously close to an unlimited undo (though not as convenient, in certain cases).

Photoshop 3.0 allows you to have up to 100 layers in a single document (99 individual layers, and the single background layer).

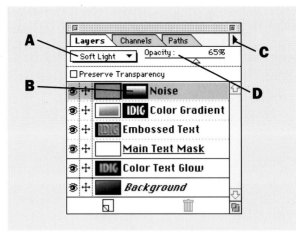

Layers are manipulated by controls in the Layers palette. There are many parameters for each layer:

A Application modes popup menu
B Layer Masks: 8-bit masks for each layer
C Layer Options popup menu
D Transparency slider

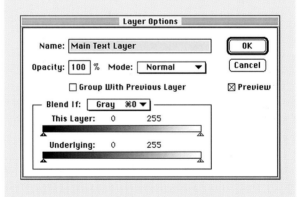

Instead of applying a paste control/composite effect once and having to live with it forever, you can now take advantage of the power of Layers and try different settings, with the ability to change things at any point along the production/creative process. Layer opacity and application mode can also be set from this dialog.

While adding layers to a document increases the overall size of the document, only the active pixels in a layer are taken into account — the surrounding transparent areas around the active pixels don't take up memory (unlike channels, which increase overall document size and RAM requirement, even if the channel consists of a single white area on a large black field). The BIG thing to watch out for though is that the current release of Photoshop has some memory flakiness when adding lots of layers to documents which are already large (100 megabytes +). *If you don't have enough RAM to accommodate the active contents of all the layers of your current document, you're likely to run into memory problems. *It's a good idea to keep a view of your active scratch disk window open in a corner of your screen, in order to interactively watch how the space is being used.*

If you've been wondering what happened to Composite Controls (called Paste Controls in earlier versions of Photoshop), fear not. Each layer has settings for exact control over the way the layer interacts with underlying layers and the background, and these controls can be found by invoking the Layer Options dialog.

Create images using layers and you'll wonder how you lived without them. Getting the most from Photoshop 3.0's layers takes some practice and slight rethinking of how you work. In the above example, we've created a fairly complex text effect using the flexibility of layers. We will study each layer individually.

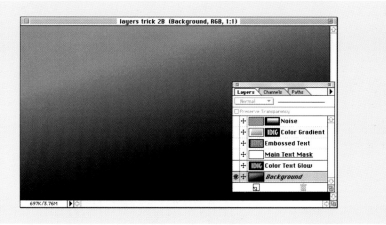

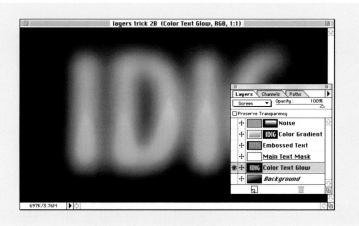

From the bottom layer up

1. Background: All documents in Photoshop 3.0 have a default background layer, which in effect is the "canvas" on which the rest of the composition occurs. A document can have only one background layer (or none). Older Photoshop documents imported into version 3.0 appear as background layers only.

2. Color Text Glow: This layer contains a blurred version of the color text layers above it. The layer is set to Screen mode, which allows it to integrate smoothly with the gradient background by combining the brightness of the two without blowing either of them to excessively bright tones.

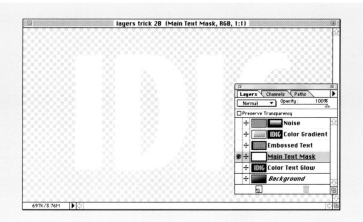

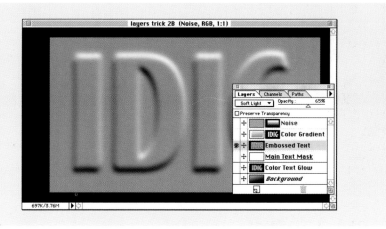

3. Main Text Mask: This layer consists of white type on a transparent background. It was created by making an empty new layer, making white the foreground color and entering type directly onto the layer. This layer is set to be the bottommost layer of a series of grouped layers above it, and acts as a clipping plane or mask for those layers (note that the clipping layer appears with its name underlined in the Layers palette). The grouped layers are visually denoted by a dotted line between them in the Layers palette.
This process is explained after the last layer is shown (page 70).

4. Embossed Text: This layer creates the 3-dimensional effect of the letters, and is created by taking the Text Mask channel (created from the previous layer) and applying Gaussian Blur and Emboss filters to create the smooth embossing effect (see chapter 31, *3D Button* on page 106 for a detailed description of this effect). The clipping effect of the previous layer puts the embossed type back into the sharp type mask.

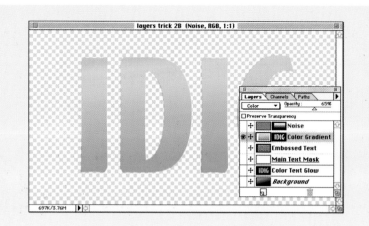

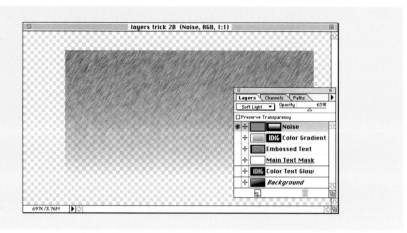

5. Color Gradient: This layer is used to colorize the embossed, masked type from the previous two layers. Made using a standard blend in Photoshop, it's being applied with the Color application mode.

6. Noise: Consisting of the Noise filter applied to a light gray or colored background, this layer adds a texture to the type effect. It's applied with 65% opacity and, in this case, the Soft Light application mode. Using different modes (such as hard and soft light) will result in significantly different texture effects on the underlying text. This layer also has a black to white gradient in the layer mask channel, which controls how the noise is laid onto underlying layers. In this example, the noise is crossfaded from full noise (top of the letters) to no noise (bottom of letters).

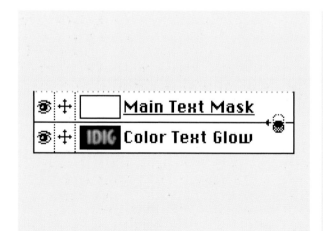

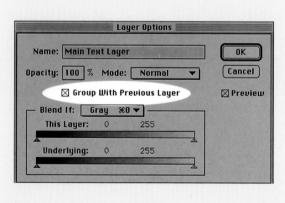

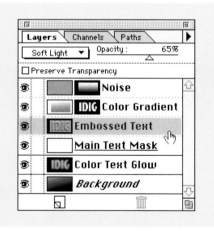

Step 3, on the previous page, mentions that the layer is acting as a clipping plane. Placing the cursor between two layers in the Layers palette, with the Option button pressed converts the cursor to the cursor shown above. Clicking between two or more layers in this fashion will make the bottom layer a mask for the ones above it. Nothing will show from the above layers except what falls within the boundaries of the contents of the layer being used to clip.

The function can be performed by double-clicking on a layer in the Layers palette and selecting Group with Previous Layer in the Layers Option dialog.

Basic layer operations

Layers can be prioritized in foreground/background space by dragging them in the Layers palette. The hierarchy is top-down: the background layer is at the bottom of the layer list, and is also the furthest object in the background. Layers on top of the background layer are in front of the background layer in the actual document.

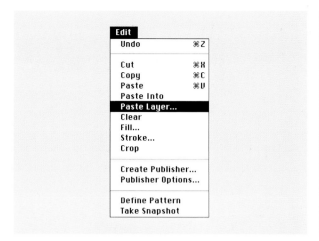

The contents of the clipboard can be pasted directly into a new layer using the Paste Layer command. If the image is smaller than the layer into which it was pasted, the remaining area of the new layer will be transparent.

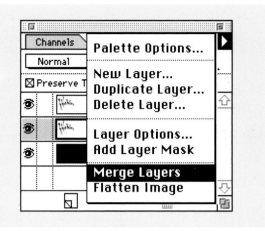

Merging layers

You can combine multiple layers into one by merging them together. ⬤ *When using the Merge Layers command, make sure that the Eye icon is turned on for the layers to be merged. Layers that are to be kept intact should be invisible (eye icon not displayed).*

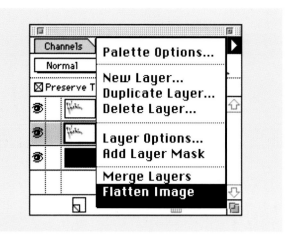

Flattening layers

The Flatten Image command in the Layers popup merges all current layers of a document.

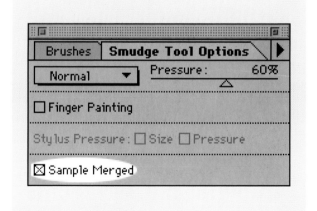

Sample Merged

Perhaps one of the most powerful options for specific tools, Sample Merged allows you to use certain tools in conjunction with layers' capabilities to achieve a neat infinite-undo effect. The tools which offer a Sample Merged option are the Magic Wand, Smudge, Blur/Sharpen tools and aligned & non-aligned Clone Rubber Stamp.

If you choose the Sample Merged option for the tools listed above and make a layer (other than the background layer) active, your effect will sample data from the background layer and will be rendered into the active layer. If you turn off the Eye icon on the background layer, you will notice that only the pixels which were modified or painted appear in the layer. The background layer remains unchanged.

Cool Layer Tricks

There are a multitude of hidden and/or not-too-obvious tricks we've run across using layers. ⬤ *You can "nudge" a layer in any direction, one pixel at a time, by using the cursor keys on your keyboard. Hold down the Shift key while pressing the cursor keys, and you'll nudge the selection 10 pixels at a time.* ⬤ *Pressing Option while clicking on a layer's Eye icon makes that layer the only visible one (all other layers turn invisible), sort of a quick "solo" option for the selected layer, or a "mute" option for all other layers.* ⬤ *Pressing Option while clicking on a Layer Mask icon (in the Layers palette) makes the layer mask visible on screen, allowing you to directly paint into the layer mask.* ⬤ *Pressing Option while positioning the cursor directly over the lines which separate layers changes the cursor and allows you to turn grouping on and off without opening each individual layer options dialog.* ⬤ *Pressing Shift while clicking on a Layer Mask*

icon causes the layer mask to be displayed in color, floating on top of the background layers (similar to Quick Mask, making an alpha channel mask visible on top of an RGB or CMYK image). ⬤ *Pressing Command while clicking on a Layer Mask icon turns the layer mask off (while retaining it for later use; the mask is not deleted).* ⬤ *Option double-clicking on a floating selection turns that selection into a new layer.* ⬤ *Pressing the numerical keys (1-9) when a layer is selected changes the opacity of the layer. Pressing 8 would set the opacity slider to 80% (yielding 20% transparency).* ⬤ *Any time you have an active selection defined anywhere in a document, you can save it directly into a layer mask. Choose Save Selection and look at the top option in the Destination Channel popup. The currently selected layer will appear as an option, and a new layer mask is created if there isn't one already defined for the layer.* ⬤ *Layers can be copied between documents using Photoshop's new drag-and-drop technology. Simply drag an active layer from one document onto the active area (NOT the Layers palette) of another document, and drop. This technique keeps the clipboard clear (very handy if you already have something in the clipboard, and don't want to lose it when copying layers between documents).*

19

Rainbow Blend

It is easy to make a two-color blend in Photoshop, but how can you make a multicolored rainbow blend, like the one found in this image? Well, it is easy, too.

We start with an image into which we will put a rainbow.

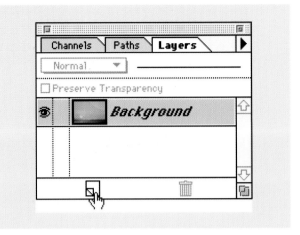

Creating a layer

1. Create a new layer by clicking the New Layer icon in the Layers palette.

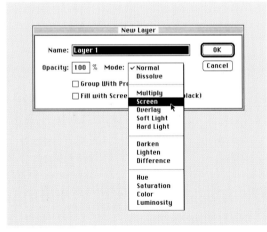

2. In the New Layer dialog box, select Screen mode.

 Screen mode looks at the color information in each channel and multiplies the inverse of the blend and base colors. The result is always a lighter color. Screening with black leaves the color unchanged. Screening with white produces white. The effect is similar to painting over an area with bleach.

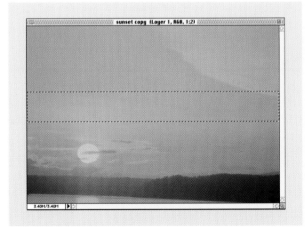

Selecting the area for the rainbow

3. With this new layer selected, use the Marquee tool to make a selection roughly the width that you want the rainbow to be.

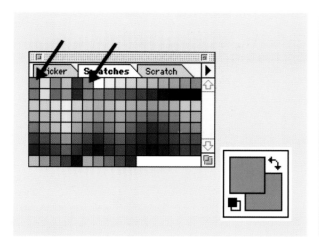

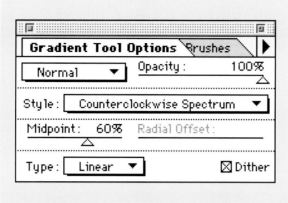

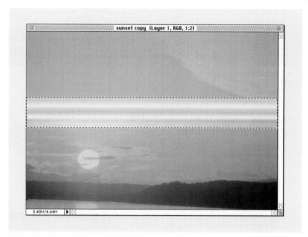

Selecting colors

4. Select the brightest red in the spectrum for foreground color, and a bright magenta for the background color.

Making the rainbow

5. Double-click the gradient tool to open the Gradient Tool Options palette. Set Style to Counterclockwise Spectrum, and set Midpoint to 60%. ⬛ *Setting the midpoint to 60% increases the amount of red in the gradient, making it look more like a rainbow.*

6. With the gradient tool selected, place the cursor at the top of the selection. Drag to the bottom of the selection, holding down the Shift key to constrain the gradient to a perfect vertical axis.

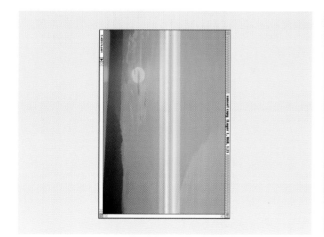

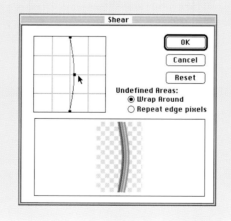

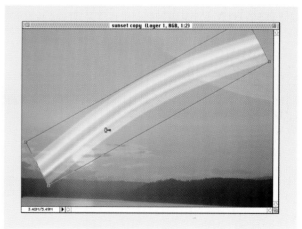

7. Press Command-D to deselect the rainbow and then rotate the entire image 90° clockwise by selecting Image> Rotate> 90° CW.

8. Run the Shear filter on the layer by choosing Filter> Distort> Shear. Move a point along the curve slightly; the preview will indicate the arc in the rainbow. Click OK.

9. Next, rotate the entire image 90° counterclockwise, by selecting Image> Rotate> 90° CCW.

10. Now choose Image> Rotate > Free. Drag one of the handles to adjust the angle of the rainbow. When the angle is as you want it, click inside the selection.

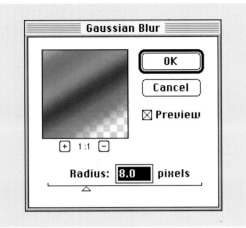

11. With the layer still selected, choose Filter> Blur> Gaussian Blur. Use a radius value that gives the rainbow a soft blur in the preview window. Then select the Move tool, and move the rainbow into its final position. ✦ *Clipped layers: If you run a filter on a layer that extends beyond the boundaries of the image, the image beyond the boundaries will be clipped off. To run a filter on this type of image, first move the entire artwork into view.*

12. Now select the Eraser tool, and erase any extra rainbow in front of your image. ✦ *Brush shortcuts: There are some great shortcuts in Photoshop for selecting brush size and opacity. The "[" key selects the next smaller brush; "]" selects the next larger; "{" selects the first brush; 1-0 changes a brush's opacity to 10 times the number (as in 2 = 20%, 0 = 100%).*

20

Retouching with Layers

Layers are the perfect venue for compositing images. In such compositions, there are effects required to add realism in the final image.

The image of the Statue of Liberty above has been updated by replacing the torch with a flashlight. A few simple layer tricks were used to complete the effect.

1. The image of the statue.

2. The image of the flashlight.

3. Using the Rotate controls found under the Image menu, the angle of the flashlight is rotated to match the angle of the original torch.

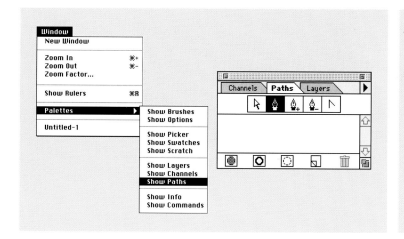

Outlining an element

4. The Path tool, located under the Palettes sub menu of the Windows menu is chosen.

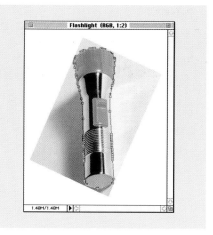

5. With the Path tool, the flashlight is outlined.

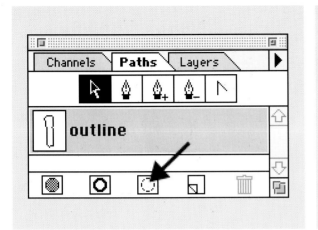

6. Once the outline is complete, it is made into a selection by dragging it over the Make Selection icon at the bottom of the Path window. It is then copied to the clipboard by pressing Command-C.

7. Back in the Statue file, the fingers are outlined in the same manner with the Path tool.

8. The outline of the fingers is turned into a selection.

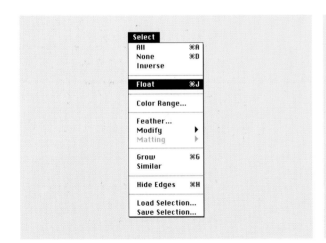

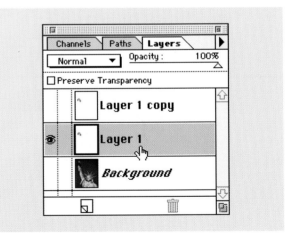

Creating a layer

9. The fingers need to be pasted into their own layer. Copying them would lose the flashlight which is currently in the clipboard. To avoid this, Float is chosen from the Select menu. This will make a copy of the selected area floating over the original without going through the clipboard.

10. In the Layers window the floating selection is shown. With the Option button pressed, double-clicking on the floating selection in the Layers window will automatically turn it into its own layer.

 Double-clicking without the Option button pressed on the floating selection in the Layers window will create a new layer but first give you the option to name it and determine its attributes. This is the same function you would get by double-clicking on an existing layer.

Making a copy of a layer

11. In the Layers window, the layer is dragged over the Document icon at the bottom of the window. This will make a copy of the layer.

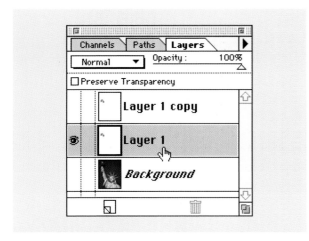

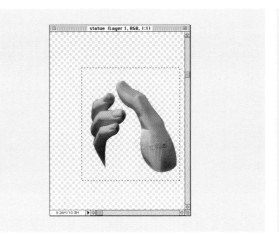

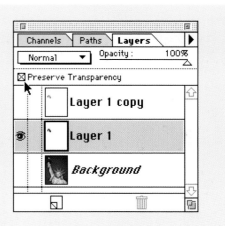

Creating a shadow

12. The original layer (Layer 1) is selected and the Eye icons of the other layer and background are turned off. This will make Layer 1 the only layer being seen and written to.

13. The area of the fingers is selected with the Rectangular Marquee tool.

14. Preserve Transparency is selected in the Layers window. This ensures that any modification done to the layer will affect only the pixels which have information.

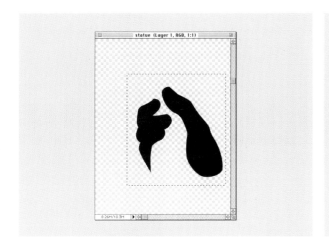

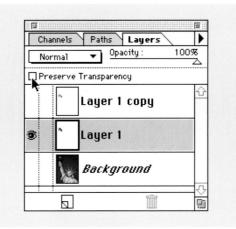

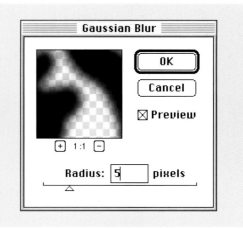

15. Black is chosen for the Foreground color and the fingers are filled with 100% black by pressing the Option and Delete keys. This layer will serve as a shadow of the original fingers.

16. The black fingers will next be blurred. Since blurs occur on both sides of an image's edge, it is necessary to turn off Preserve Transparency.

17. Gaussian Blur is chosen from the Blur sub menu of the Filters menu. In the dialog box an amount is entered to get the desired result.

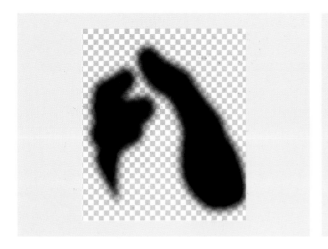

The result looks like the image shown above.

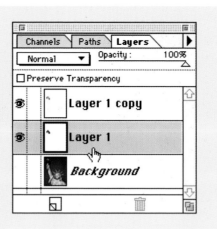

18. The Eye icon is turned on for the layer which contains the green fingers. The layer with the black fingers is still the highlighted one being written to.

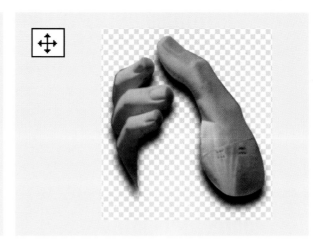

19. Using the Move tool, the black, blurred fingers are moved down a bit to give the appearance of a shadow.

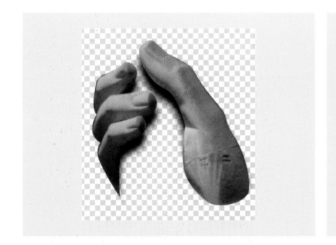

20. With the Eraser tool, the sections of the shadow which appear in an area where such a shadow would not be cast are eliminated.

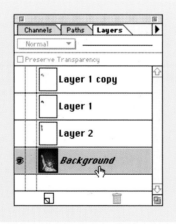

Retouching the background

21. The background layer is selected.

22. Using the Clone tool, portions of the sky are cloned over the original torch to erase it from the image.

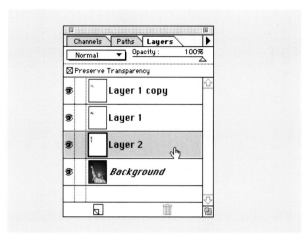

23. The flashlight, which is still in the clipboard, is now brought into the image. Paste Layer is chosen from the Edit menu.

Colorizing the flashlight

24. The area of the flashlight is selected with the Rectangular Marquee tool. Preserve transparency is turned on in the Layers window.

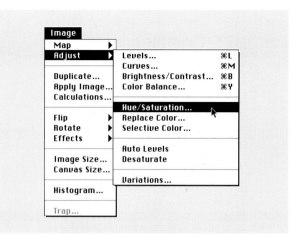

25. Hue/Saturation is selected from the Adjust sub menu of the Image menu.

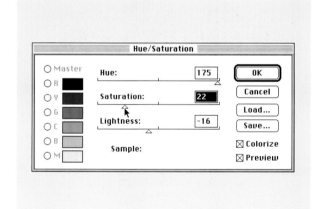

The Colorize option is selected and the Hue slider is moved to a range which matches the statue. The Saturation is brought down to dull the color.

The result is a flashlight which seems to be made of the same material as the statue. The statue has been updated!

21

Drop Shadows Using Layers

Drop shadows are easier to create using layers in Photoshop 3.0.

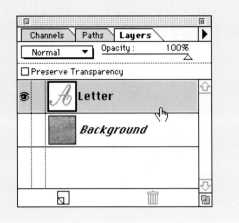

In this example, the letter A is on its own layer (Letter).

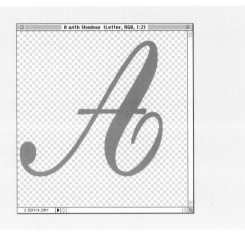

The area around the character is transparent, indicated by the gray checkerboard, allowing the background to show through.

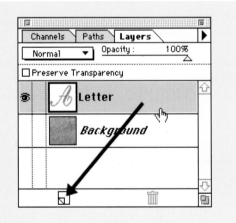

Making a copy of a layer

1. Make a copy of the first layer (letter) by dragging the layer name to the New Layer icon at the bottom of the palette. This copy (letter copy) is placed on top of the original layer. ● *The active layer is shown in gray on the Macintosh and in white on Windows. The Eye icons let you turn layers on and off.*

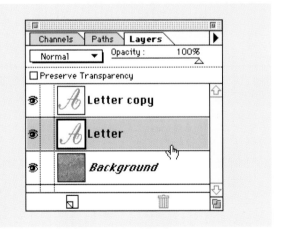

2. Select the original letter layer in the palette.

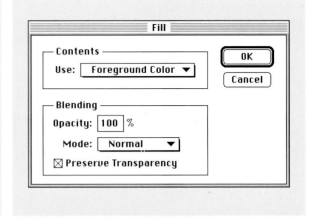

Moving the layer

With the Move tool, offset the layer to the lower right or wherever you want the shadow to appear (the layer being moved is underneath the copy.) Only the outline of the image shows when being moved. After moving, the image regains its color when the mouse button is released.

3. Release the mouse button when the layer is slightly offset. This will become the drop shadow. At this stage, it is the same color as the letter casting the shadow. This is because it is simply a copy of itself.

4. Select Fill from the Edit menu, select Preserve Transparency, and fill using the foreground color.

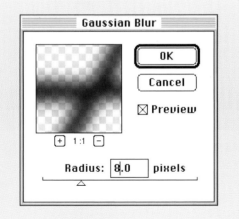

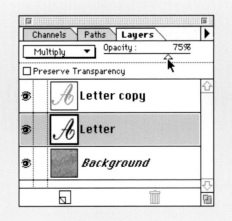

5. Use the Gaussian Blur filter (Filter>Blur>Gaussian Blur) to soften the shadow. Here we used a radius of 8 for a 300-ppi image. For higher or lower resolution images, you will need to use a higher or lower radius value. Note: Before applying the filter, make sure Preserve Transparency is turned off in the Layers palette.

6. Combine the drop shadow with the background using the Multiply mode in the Layers palette. The effect can be further softened by reducing the opacity of the layer. ● *The Multiply mode is the equivalent of placing two transparencies over each other and viewing them illuminated by a light table. The result is a darker combination of the two images.*

22

Complex Shadows Using Layers

The previous exercise demonstrated a simple technique for creating drop shadows. Shadows add depth to an image. Shadows are also necessary to add realism. The image shown here is realistic enough only because the shadow ties the man into the scene.

The football player is one image.

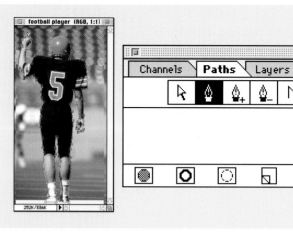

Outlining element

1. Using the Path tool, the player is outlined.

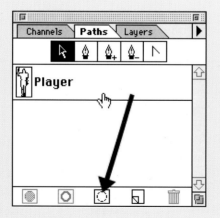

Making path a selection

2. The path is turned into a selection by dragging it over the Make Selection icon at the bottom of the Paths palette.

3. The file of the wall in front of which the player will stand is opened.

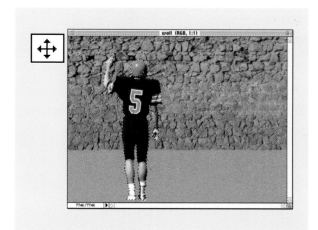

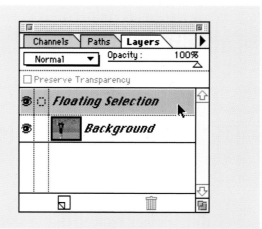

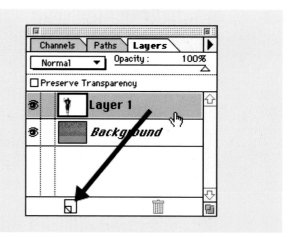

4. The selected player is copied over to the wall image using the Move tool.

5. In the Layers palette, the player appears as a Floating Selection. Double-clicking on the Floating Selection in the palette with the Option button pressed will automatically put it into a layer. ⬤ *The same action without the Option button pressed will make a layer but first pop up the Layer Options window.*

6. Two copies of the layer are made by dragging the layer over the Document icon at the bottom of the palette twice.

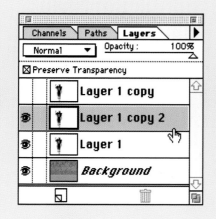

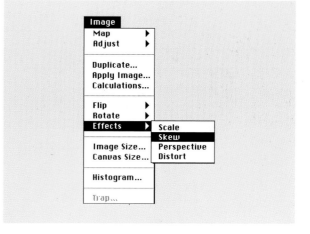

7. The top layer will be the athlete while the two layers below it will serve to make the shadow. The first of the two lower layers is selected to write to and Preserve Transparency is turned on. The Eye icon for the top layer is turned off. ⬤ *Copies of layers always come in above the layer being copied, thus appearing in front of the original layer.*

8. With the Foreground color black, the Option and Delete keys are pressed to fill the layer with 100% black. ⬤ *Preserve Transparency limits the fill to the pixels in the layer which have information, thus affecting only the player, leaving the rest of the layer transparent.*

9. The same is done to the other layer at the bottom.

10. The Skew function is called up.

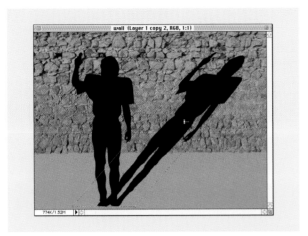

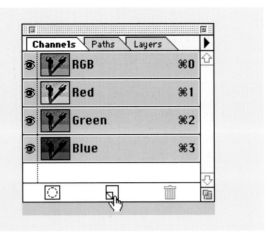

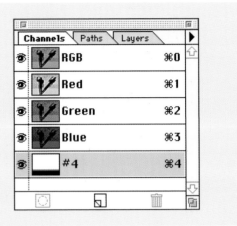

11. One of the shadow layers is skewed to form the shadow which is cast along the ground.

12. An alpha channel is created by clicking the Document icon in the Channels palette.

13. Turn the Eye icon on to view the RGB over the Alpha channel. The alpha channel is made active. With the Gradient tool, a blend from black to white is made which covers the area of the ground where the shadow is cast.

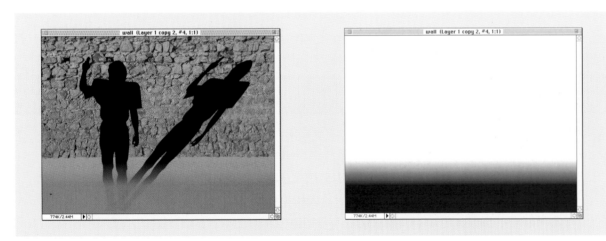

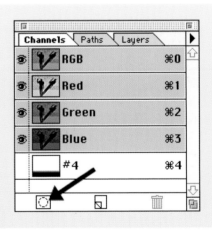

As a shadow moves away from the source it fades. In the next step this effect will be accomplished using this Alpha channel.

14. The alpha channel is made a selection by dragging it over the Make Selection icon at the bottom of the Channels palette. At this point the Eye icon of the alpha channel can be turned off. The RGB is made the active channel.

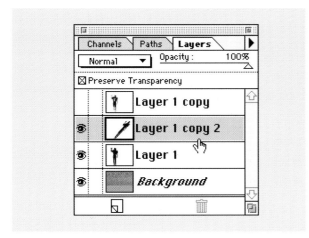

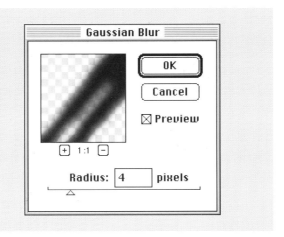

15. The skewed layer is made active and Preserve Transparency is turned off.

16. The Gaussian Blur filter is called up. An amount is entered which gives the best result, in this case, 4.

17. Using the Eraser tool, the section of the shadow which falls on the wall is erased.

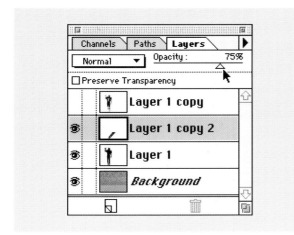

18. Finally, the Opacity for the layer is lowered.

19. The second shadow layer is made active. Preserve Transparency is turned off and it is blurred using the same setting as the other shadow. It is then moved to match up the edge where the other shadow left off.

20. The portion of the shadow that extends below the wall is erased and the opacity is brought down. The result is a realistic scene.

23

Global Layer Adjustments

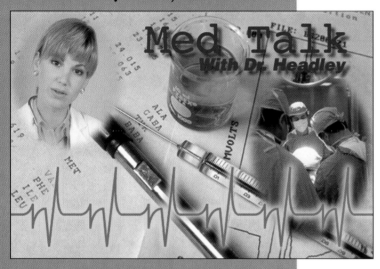

Currently, it is not possible to make overall image adjustments to a layered document. Adjustments affect only the layer that is selected. This super technique shows a simple solution that lets you control all layers in appearance to the image. This is a handy trick when adjustments in brightness, color or any other overall modification is necessary without the need to lose the layers.

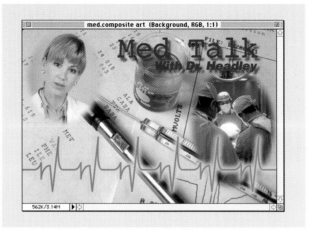

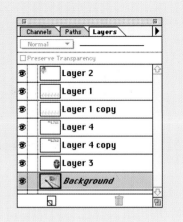

The image above is comprised of a background and six elements (text, text shadow, etc.)

Each element is in its own layer. We will now adjust all the layers together.

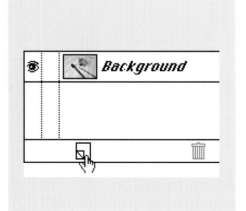

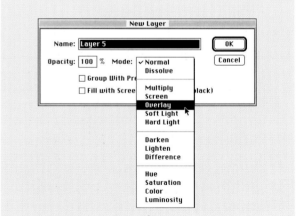

1. First create a new layer that will sit on top of all other layers by clicking the New Layer icon in the Layers palette.

2. In the New Layer dialog box, select the Overlay mode.

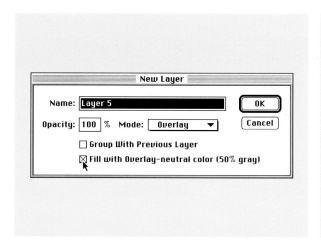

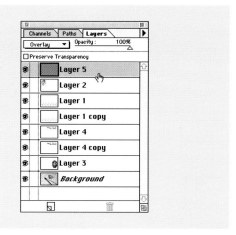

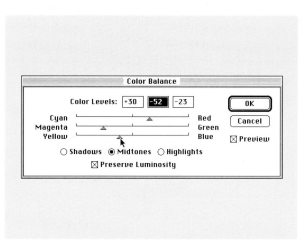

3. Select Fill with Overlay-neutral color (50% gray). This makes the background of the new overlay layer neutral—that is, transparent.

4. Select this new layer in the Layers palette.

5. Press Command-Y to bring up the Color Balance dialog box. Adjust the color balance for the layer. Because this layer is in Overlay mode, it affects the appearance of all layers below it. It does not change the layers; it merely tints them.

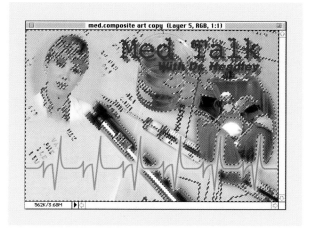

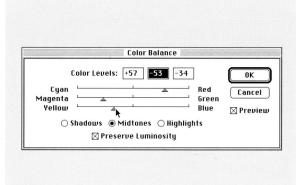

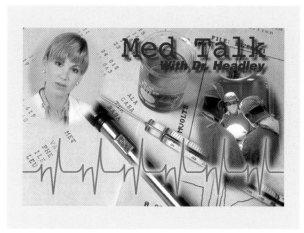

6. To apply color changes to only the highlights of the image, undo step 3 (Command-Z), and then press Command-Option-0 to load the luminosity values for the entire image. ⬢ *Loading the luminosity values as a selection lets you easily adjust just the highlights in an image.*

7. Press Command-Y to display the Color Balance dialog box, and adjust the sliders as desired. ⬢ *To reload the last used settings in Color Balance, press Command-Option-Y. Using the Option key to open a dialog box reloads the last used settings for many other controls in Photoshop, such as Hue/Saturation, Replace Color, and Levels.*

8. Press Command-D to deselect the image. The slightly warmer tone given to the overlay layer affects all the layers below. There you have it—global layer adjustments to an entire image, without altering the individual layers.

24

Wet Glass Effect

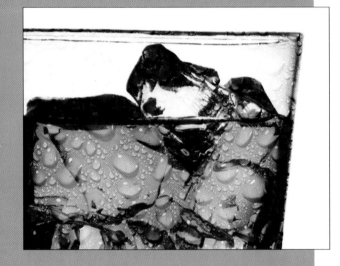

The various modes available to the layers opens the door to a fountain of special effects as well as solutions to some everyday problems.

The job here called for an image of a wet glass of scotch.

1. An image of a glass of scotch was available but it wasn't wet.

2. We did, however, have an additional image which was a background of water droplets.

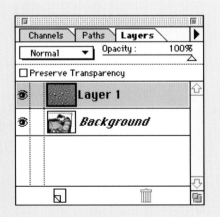

3. We opened both files in Photoshop. Using the Move tool, the image of the water drops was dragged over the image of the glass. This drops a copy of the water drops automatically into a new layer in the glass image.

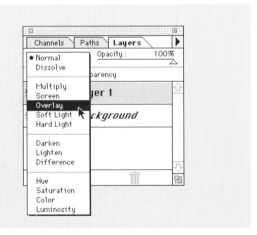

4. In the Layers palette, the mode of the layer is changed to Overlay. The result is a wet-looking glass.

25

Color Correction

Photoshop 3.0 offers many ways to do color correction. The Adjust sub menu, under the Image menu, contains controls for manipulating the luminosity, saturation and all the color attributes of an image.

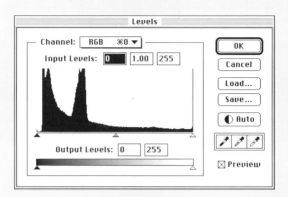

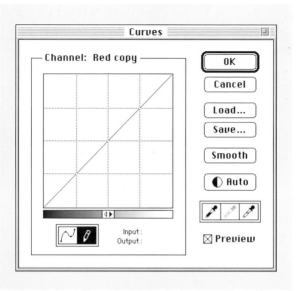

Levels

The first thing that is clearly visible when the Levels dialog box opens is what makes Levels such a precise tool — a histogram. The histogram is a chart, displaying the number of pixels at each level of brightness. The horizontal axis of the chart represents brightness, with black on the left and white on the right, while the vertical axis represents the number of pixels in the image at a certain brightness level.

The input values indicate the current density of the various brightness levels. The sliders underneath can increase the contrast if pulled inward. The black slider specifies what value is 100% black (the "black point"), the gray slider at the center manipulates the midtone values (or gamma), the white slider at the right sets the 100% white value (the "white point"). Values can also be entered into the Input Levels text boxes, or by designating the black and white points in the image itself with the Eyedropper tool set in the lower right corner. The Auto button defines the lightest and darkest values in an image as black and white and then redistributes the remaining values evenly between the two end values. You can also use the Eyedropper tools in the Levels dialog to visually select specific areas of colors in the actual image document to be processed as the black, mid and highlight values.

The output levels, visible at the bottom of the dialog box, decrease the contrast of the image by limiting the range of blacks and whites represented in the image.

In Levels you can work globally or in a particular channel.

Curves

Like Levels, Curves allows you to adjust the tonal ranges in an image. Here, you are not limited to the midtones, highlight and shadows but instead, can adjust any point along a gray-level scale while keeping other levels constant or proportionally restrained. Like any other adjustments, Curves can be used globally (to a combined RGB image) or to individual color channels.

If you drag the cursor out onto the main image document display and click the mouse button, the currently selected value will appear highlighted in the Curves dialog by a "bouncing ball" indicator. Darker values appear on the lower left starting with black, which has a value of 0. The scale is in ascending order to the lighter values on the upper right, ending in white, which has a value of 255. Each row or column in the grid represents 64 steps in the scale. The diagonal line shows the current relationship, with every pixel having the same input and output value. Placing a point anywhere on the diagonal line and dragging it allows you to increase or decrease its value.

Using the Pencil tool in the dialog box, you can reposition pixel values. This function is known as the Arbitrary Map. There is an Auto button which works approximately the same way it does in the Levels dialog box.

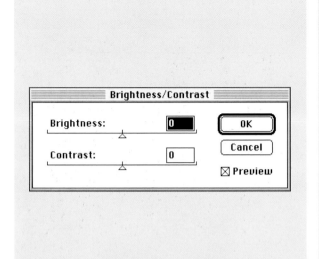

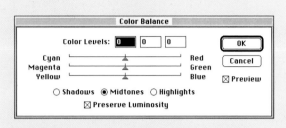

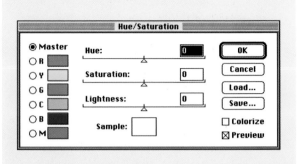

Brightness/Contrast

Brightness/Contrast is the brute force method of tonal control. It lacks a visual histogram and the finer control afforded by the Input and Output sliders and eyedropper tools. Don't use it—learn to use Levels and Curves instead.

Color Balance

Color Balance gives you the ability to change the hue and saturation of the colors in your image. You can work with shadows, midtones and highlights separately. To use these controls, you choose which value, shadows, etc., you want to modify and then move the sliders toward the colors you want to make stronger. To reduce a certain color, you drag the slider away from that color.

There is a Preserve Luminosity choice at the bottom of the dialog box which is useful to maintain the overall brightness balance of the image, while allowing overall color tone changes to be made.

Hue/Saturation

This command lets you change the hue, saturation and intensity of color values in an image.

- Hue is color tonality; spectrum absorption.
- Saturation is the purity, or intensity of color.
- Lightness is blending hue and saturation with white or brightness.

The color swatches on the left of the dialog allow you to determine before/after color instances, as well as isolate specific color ranges in the image to be affected.

The Colorize option lets you adjust the values of the entire image to a set value. A very fast way to tint an image interactively.

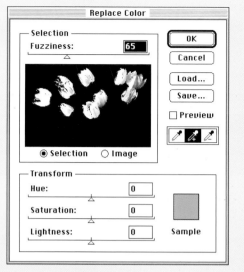

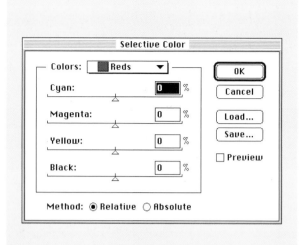

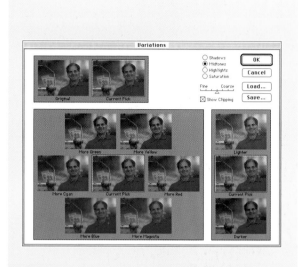

Replace Color

Replace Color gives you control over certain tonal/color values which you visually select from the image. It is a one-stop control for isolating a specific color in an image and replacing it with another color.

 The functionality of Replace Color can be largely duplicated using the Color Range command (Select>Color Range) to create an editable alpha channel for a color, and using it as a mask with any other Photoshop color correction tools. Replace color is more straightforward, but in some ways more constraining.

By dragging the cursor over values displayed in the preview image in the Replace Color dialog box, those values become selected within the Replace Color command. The Fuzziness slider at the top allows you to increase the range of the chosen values to be modified. The sliders at the bottom function the same way as they do in Hue/Saturation, but in this case are applied only to the values currently selected in the Replace Color command.

Selective Color

Selective Color allows you to modify a color by changing the amount of ink that is used to make a particular color. This form of color correcting is prepress specific. The color range is selected at the top of the box; moving the sliders which correspond to the printing inks at the bottom of the box will make the necessary adjustments

Auto Levels

Auto Levels works precisely the same way the Auto buttons do in the Levels and Curves dialog boxes. It defines the lightest and darkest values in an image as black and white and then redistributes the remaining values evenly between the two end values. The user cannot specify any parameters using this setting.

Desaturate

Desaturate removes the saturation value of all the colors in the image, resulting in a grayscale image, but the image remains an RGB image.

Variations

Variations lets you visually adjust color balance, contrast and saturation of an image or selection. You can work on shadows, midtones, highlights and saturation separately. At the top of the dialog box there are two previews of the current image or selected portion. One preview remains the same and represents the original. The second shows the current adjustment in Variations and lets you compare it to the original. Throughout the dialog box are many other previews of the image which give you an advance look at what any particular adjustment will do to the image. When an adjustment is made by simply clicking on the preview that's closer to what you want, all the previews update themselves to reflect the new state of the image.

The Clipping toggle will display areas that are out of the print reproduction gamut. The goal is to make the Clipping toggle show nothing on the image displays, which means all colors will reproduce properly.

26

Overexposure Correction with Layers

A common problem which occurs with photographic images is overexposure. This happens when the photographic film is exposed to light for longer than desired, resulting in an image which is far too bright and which has blown out highlights (the brighter areas of the image wash out to white). One approach to fixing an overexposed image would be to use Photoshop's Levels or Curve controls to adjust overall densities in the image. But there is a better way: using copies of the overexposed image on separate layers, with intelligent use of the Multiply application mode.

1. Open the overexposed image, which will come in as a background layer by default.

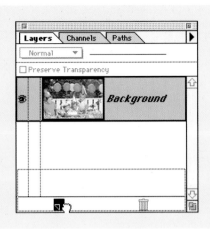

2. Copy the background layer by dragging the background layer onto the New Layer icon at the bottom of the Layers palette.

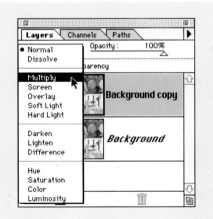

3. The new layer is selected by default. Choose Multiply from the transfer mode popup menu in the Layers palette. Look at the resulting image—the dark densities have built up quite nicely, resulting in a more balanced overall image. The multiply transfer mode builds up dark densities in proportional amounts, without "overdriving" pixel brightness.

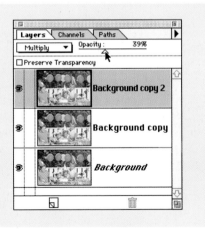

4. Let's say that the image derived in step 3 still isn't dark enough; simply copy the layer created in step 2 by dragging it onto the New Layer icon. The entire image will now get even darker—in fact, too much so (notice that leaves in the background are beginning to lose detail). This can be fixed by adjusting the opacity of the new copy. With the new layer copy selected, drag the Opacity slider in the Layers palette to a lower value. The opacity of any Layer except the background layer can be adjusted until the desired density value is achieved.

27

Variations

Even though there are many different tools for doing color correction work in Photoshop, the Variations tool is perhaps the most intuitive and interactive choice for many color correction tasks. The trick to getting the most from Variations is knowing how to "read" the interface, which involves learning a little about the arrangement of the controls.

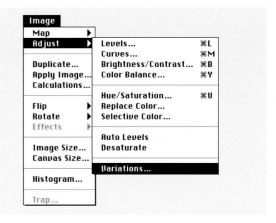

1. Open an image which has a clear color cast and other color imperfections. This example contains a very strong blue cast and is darker than it should be for optimum reproduction.

2. Open the Variations color correction module by selecting Image>Adjust>Variations.

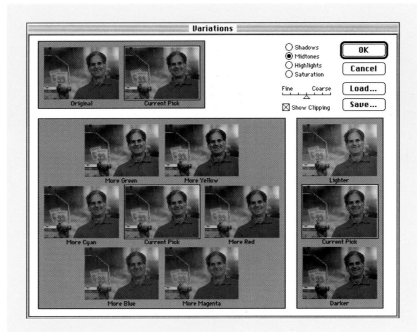

3. Variations displays a visual array of different permutations of the selected area (or whole image, if nothing is selected). Let's look more closely at the different controls in the Variations dialog.

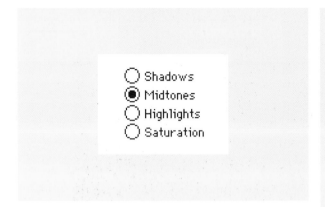

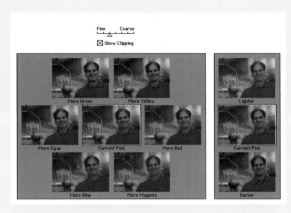

4. To the right of the dialog are controls for choosing whether you're predominantly affecting the shadow, midtone, highlights or saturation values of the image. Most overall color corrections take place in the midtones (especially in the case of color casts), while the shadow and highlight buttons are used to isolate and affect colors in the darkest and lightest areas of an image, respectively. For this example, we'll go with the Midtones radio button selected. The saturation control is used to selectively add or subtract color saturation from the image.

5. The slider control found under the radio buttons mentioned in the previous step allows you to determine the amount of color shifting applied to the color permutations in the Variations dialog. If the slider is moved closer to Fine, the amount of difference between the variations is much lower, while sliding the control toward Coarse increases the difference between the variations. A good general color correction strategy is to use coarser settings to get into the general ballpark, then move the slider toward a finer setting to fine-tune the corrections.

6. Now to the main subject: how to "read" the settings to make color correction tasks even easier, and take advantage of the arrangement of the variations thumbnails. If you look at the color variations thumbnails in the lower left portion of the Variations dialog, note that the choices are labeled More Yellow, More Red and so on. This means that if you click on that thumbnail, then the corresponding color component is added to the image. While the placement of these More Color thumbnails appears arbitrary, it's not true: there is a design to the arrangement. ❤ *The trick is to "see" what we call the "Star," which links complementary colors together. In the case of the example image, we know that there's a heavy blue cast, so we find the More Blue thumbnail and follow the star straight across (no turns allowed!) to find that More Yellow is the direction we want to take the image. Following this rule, we also see that Green and Magenta are opposites, as are Red and Cyan.*

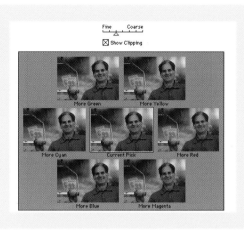

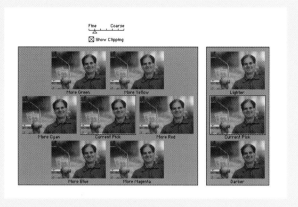

7. Click on the More Yellow thumbnail, and all of the previews update. The image in the center of the star is the currently processed version (with all of the changes made since you opened the Variations dialog), and as you can see, is much closer to looking acceptable.

8. But note that all of the other color previews are too extreme; it's time to adjust the Increment slider to be closer to Fine, which shows much more subtle variations of the image. The center image now appears to have a soft cyan cast, so we follow the star and click on the More Red. We then adjust the slider down one more notch toward Fine and click on More Red once more. While we could spend more time on this image, you can see that with just a few mouse clicks we've turned the previously horrific colors toward something much more acceptable and useful. We could click on the Darker and Lighter thumbnails on the right side of the dialog to tune in better brightness values until we get a perfect colored image.

 If you decide that you have made some wrong moves in Variations and want to start over, you can always click on the Original thumbnail in the upper left corner to reset everything back to the state it was in when Variations was first invoked.

The result is an image which has been properly color corected.

28

Interactive Inline Type

Inline text effects have always been fairly difficult to achieve in Photoshop, yet very simple to create in Adobe Illustrator. The basic idea behind inline type is to create multiple copies of some type, make each copy a different color and thickness value, and lay the copies on top of each other, in order to get a layered, multiple-outline effect.

This trick can now be accomplished easily in Photoshop, without all of the manual steps involved in creating similar effects in Illustrator, with the added benefit of being able to change the inlining characteristics in real-time, until you get the exact desired result.

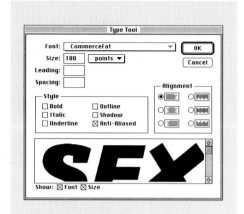

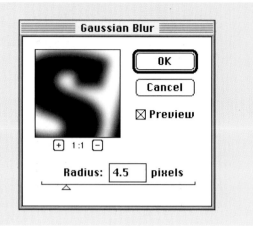

Creating type
1. Create some black type in an RGB document with a white background. This technique tends to work better with larger type sizes. Make sure to turn on the Anti-Aliased checkbox in the Style section of the dialog box.

Blurring the type
2. Apply some blurring to the type and the background using the Gaussian Blur filter. More blurring will result in more predominant inlining, but too much blurring will erode the final letter forms. Try Gaussian Blur values between 3 and 7 pixels (more if the image is higher resolution).

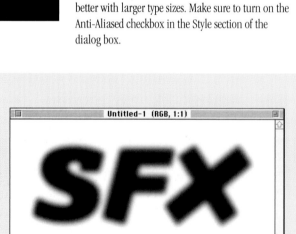

The result should look somewhat like the example above.

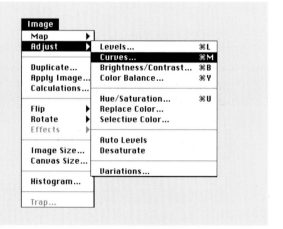

Creating inline effect
3. Open the Curves dialog (Image>Adjust>Curves...).

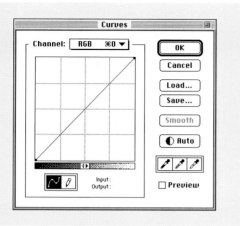

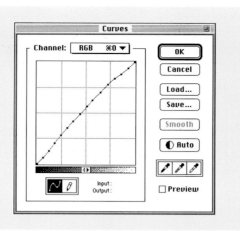

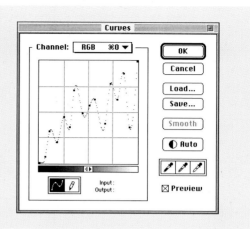

The dialog box will pop up. Make sure that Curves is set to curves (and not arbitrary map mode) by clicking on the spline icon at the bottom of the dialog (this is usually the default mode for the Curves command).

4. Create new curve control points by clicking along the transfer curve in the central area of the dialog. Place enough control points to cover the entire length of the transfer curve; larger numbers of control points will result in more intricate inline effects.

5. Now comes the fun part. Making sure that the preview button is checked, try dragging alternating control points up and down, while looking at the blurred type in the background. As you drag the points, you'll see outlines appear on the edges of the type. If you drag a point up, light lines appear, while darker lines appear when dragging points down.

The left part of the transfer curve affects the inside of the blurred area, while the right portion of the curve affects the outside edges of the type.

6. You can use the resulting inline type by itself, or by inverting the image, you can use the type as an alpha channel for creating more diverse type effects.

29

Metallic Type

One of the most popular effects is metallic type. 3D programs allow you to extrude type and apply a metallic texture to it. A disadvantage is the rendering time required in 3D programs to produce the finished art. Another disadvantage is that you may not own a 3D program. Here is an easy way to achieve the effect using Photoshop.

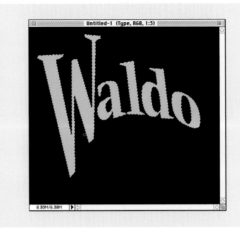

To start, Illustrator was used to create this stylized type. You can do something similar or use straight type.

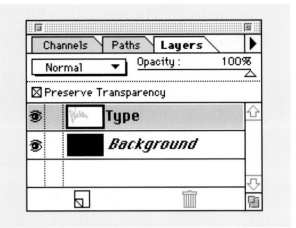

Importing Illustrator file
1. The Illustrator file was Placed into the Photoshop file using the Place command found under the File menu and saved into its own layer. That layer is selected.

Making a selection
2. Option-Command-T is pressed. This uses the transparency in the layer to make a selection of the active pixels.

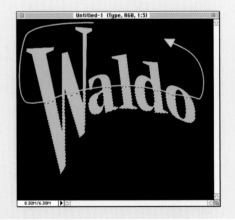

Deselecting the top of the type
3. Using the Lasso tool with the Command key pressed to deselect, the upper portion of the selected type is surrounded to subtract it from the selection.

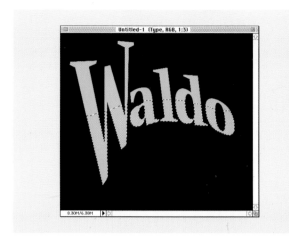

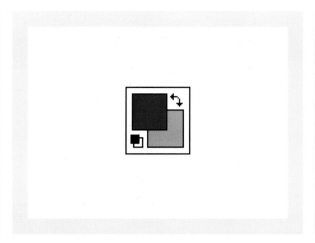

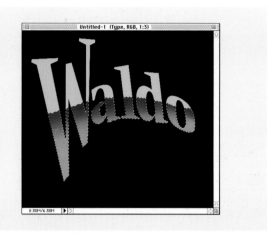

The result is the lower area remains selected.

Selecting colors
4. Dark and light earth tones are chosen for the foreground and background colors.

Dropping in the blend
5. With the Gradient tool, a gradient is applied with the dark tone at the top of the selected area ending in the lighter tone towards the bottom.

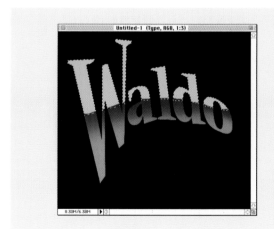

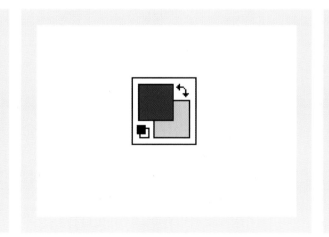

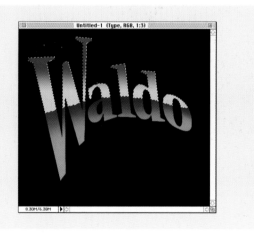

6. Option-Command-T is pressed again. This time with the Lasso tool and the Command key pressed to deselect, the lower portion of the selected type, which was filled with the blend, is surrounded to subtract it from the selection.

7. A blue range of colors to simulate a sky are chosen.

8. With the Gradient tool, a gradient is applied with the dark tone at the top of the selected area ending in the lighter tone toward the bottom.

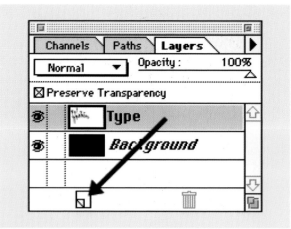

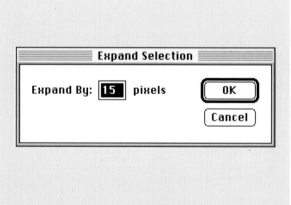

9. Option-Command-T is pressed again.

10. With the Paintbrush tool and black for the color, a simulation of a mountain range is painted where the two blends meet.

Creating edge

11. A copy of the type layer is made by dragging the layer's icon over the Document icon at the bottom of the Layers palette.

12. The first layer is selected.

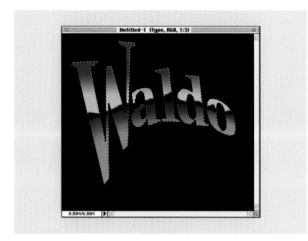

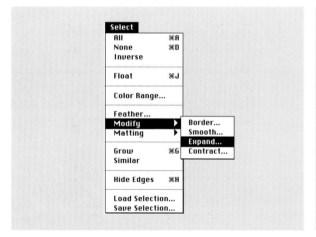

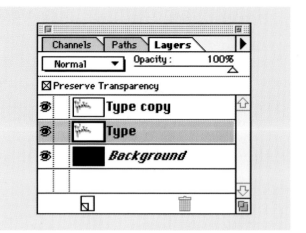

13. Option-Command-T is pressed again.

14. Expand is chosen from the Modify sub menu of the Select menu.

15. In the dialog box that appears, an amount is entered to create an edge around the type.

The result should look like the example shown above.

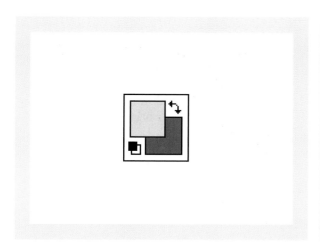

Coloring the edge
16. A range of grays is chosen for the colors.

17. With the Gradient tool, a gradient is applied with the dark tone at the top of the selected area ending in the lighter tone toward the bottom.

18. With the Airbrush tool, using various sizes and shades of gray, highlights are added to the edges.

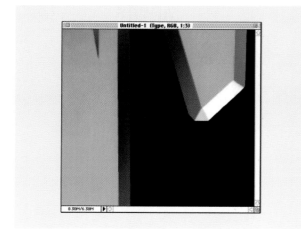

Extra details can be added to the corners.

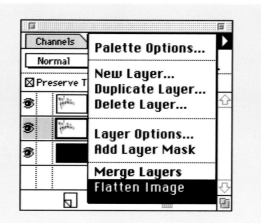

Flattening the layers
19. The layers are now flattened into the background.

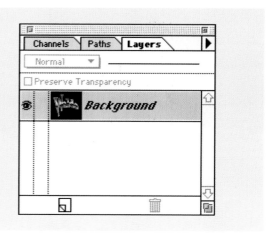

This will create a single image layer.

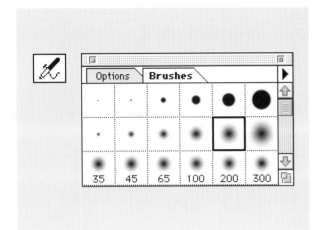

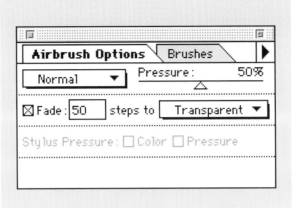

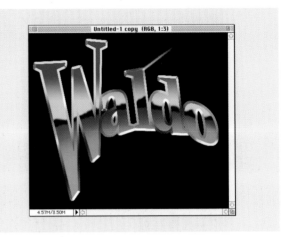

Creating a sparkle

20. The Airbrush is chosen and assigned a size which will serve to create a sparkle effect.

21. In the Airbrush Options, Fade is selected with an amount to create a small streak.

22. With white for the color, a single click is performed over an edge of the type. In this case, the top of the L was done. With the Shift key pressed, a second click is done at the outer edges of the image.

 The Shift key constrains the clicks to each other.

Note: *If a Fade number has been set, it is important to have the second, connecting click, fall beyond the distance of the Fade in order for the streak to completely fade out.*

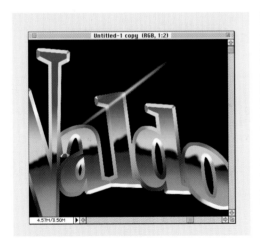

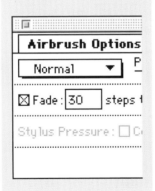

23. Without the Shift key, click again on the letter where the first click was performed. Now, with the Shift key pressed, click to the bottom keeping a straight line with the first streak.

24. The Fade amount is lowered.

25. Without the Shift key, click again on the letter where the first click was performed. Now, with the Shift key pressed, click in a direction which is perpendicular to the first streak.

26. As in step 24, create a second small streak in the opposite direction of the first.

30

Soft Embossing

While anyone can use the standard Photoshop emboss filter to create embossing effects with graphics, the fact is that there's a trick to achieving smooth, slick embossing effects. Let's take a look at using this technique to create some smooth embossed type.

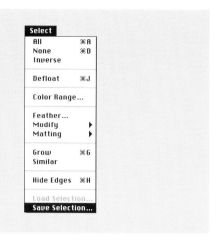

1. Create some type using the Text tool. For this exercise, try using a larger (90 pixels or more) size on a blank RGB document. Use anti-aliasing.

2. Making sure that the new type is still selected, save the selection as an alpha channel (choose Selection>Save Selection...).

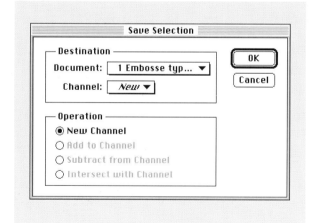

Save the selection into a New Channel in the same document.

3. Using the Rectangular Marquee tool, select the type and a decent amount of area surrounding the type.

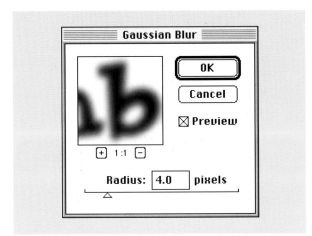

4. Choose Filter>Blur>Gaussian Blur. Higher pixel radius values will yield smoother edges on the final embossed type. For this example, we'll use a radius of 4. Click OK.

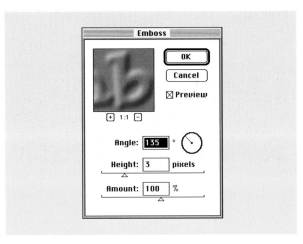

5. Choose Filter>Stylize>Emboss. Try using the default values (as shown). Click OK.

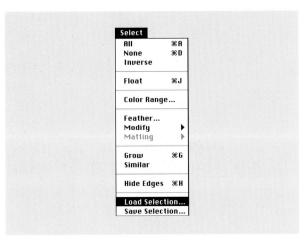

6. Now that we've got some nice, smooth embossed type, the final step is to use the alpha channel created in step #2 as a mask to select the embossed type. Choose Selection>Load Selection.

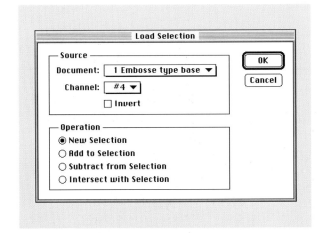

Load Channel #4 as a New Selection.

7. With the embossed type selected, copy and paste the type into the desired background.

The results can be quite spectacular.

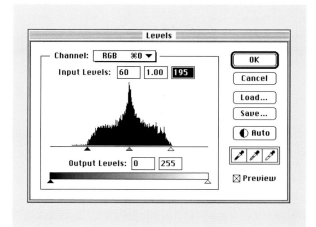

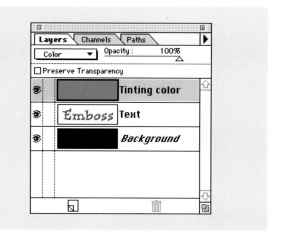

8. If the emboss effect looks too subtle, try adjusting the type using the Levels command (Image>Adjust>Levels). An optimum Levels adjustment for the embossed type looks like the one shown here.

Once processed with this Levels adjustment, the embossed type has much more "punch."

9. You can colorize the embossed type by placing the type in one layer, and creating a new layer above it, filled with color and set to a tinting application mode. In this example, the type (in the middle layer) is placed on a black background, and a new layer is created on top of the type, filled with blue, and set to Color mode.

The result is type which is colorized.

31

Quick & Easy 3D Buttons

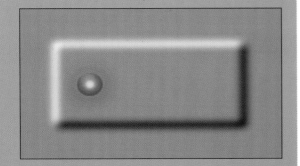

Regardless of the type of multimedia productions you produce, one of the design elements that you'll almost always need to incorporate is buttons. One of the telltale signs of a glitzy multimedia interface is 3D buttons. While many artists invariably turn to 3D software to make the most basic of 3D shapes, it's quite simple to quickly cook up some 3D buttons in Photoshop and easily transfer them over to an interactive animation program. In this lesson, you'll learn the trick to easily making 3D beveled effects in Photoshop, and to add a nifty glowing LED (Light Emitting Diode) which lights up when the button is pressed.

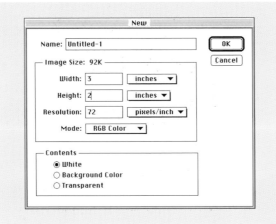

1. In Photoshop, make a new RGB document. For this example, we've made a 3x2 inch document; make the document just a bit larger than the intended button size. Make sure the background color is set to white.

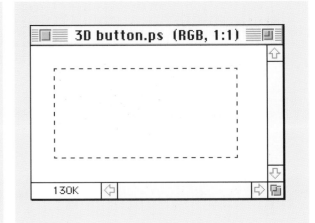

2. With the Rectangular Marquee, select an area to correspond to the general button shape as shown above. If you want a round button, then simply use the Circular Marquee; odd shaped buttons can be made by making selections with the Lasso (using the option key, to constrain the lasso to straight lines for polygonal shapes). Save the selection by choosing Select>Save Selection>New (resulting in a new alpha channel).

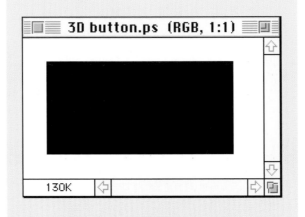

3. Load the new channel onto the blank, white RGB document as a selection (Select>Load Selection). Fill the selection with black.
🍎 *This can be quickly done by making black the foreground color and pressing the option and delete keys simultaneously.*
You should now be looking at a black rectangle against a white background in the RGB channels as shown above.

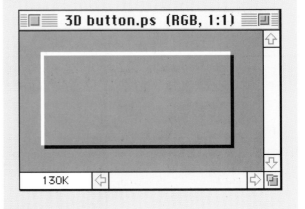

4. Now comes the fun part: in order to create a true 3D effect, we'll use a combination of the Gaussian Blur and Emboss filters. If you've tried embossing a straight black and white image (like black text on a white background), you'll rarely find the results appealing—it simply looks like a gray box with a thick black outline on one side and a white border on the other side, like the sample above.

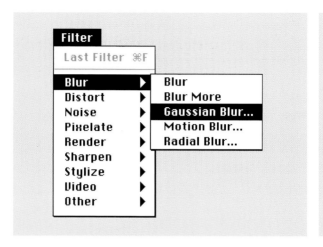

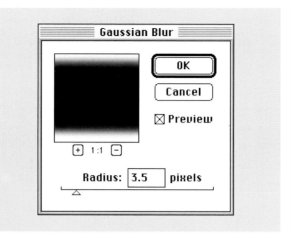

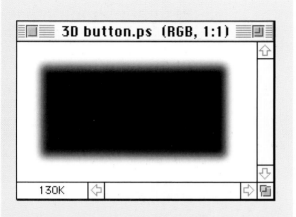

5. The trick to smooth embossing is to blur the image before embossing it (this trick also works wonders for creating 3D embossed text). Select the entire RGB document (Select>Select All) and choose the Gaussian Blur filter (Filter>Blur>Gaussian Blur).

6. For this example, we'll use a setting of 3.5 pixels.

The result should look like the example above.

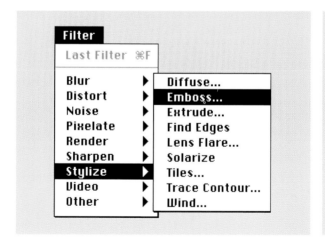

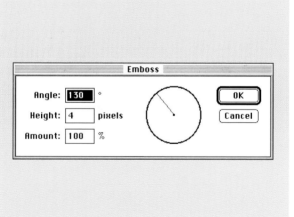

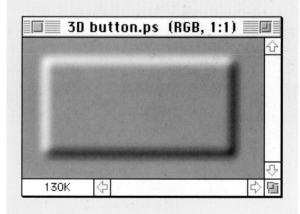

7. Once the blurring is complete, choose the Emboss filter (Stylize>Emboss).

8. Set the parameters to those shown above.

Once the image is embossed, you'll clearly see the 3D effect on the edges of the square.

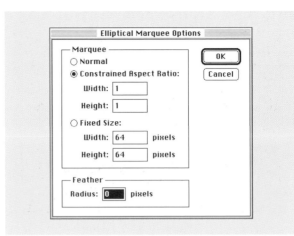

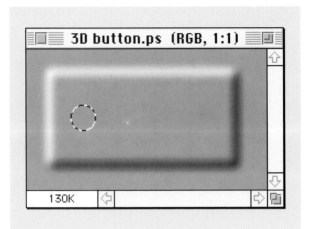

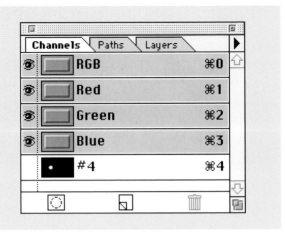

9. Now it's time to make the LED. Option-click the Marquee tool to convert it from the Rectangular to the Circular tool. Double click on the Circular Marquee tool, which brings up the options for the tool; select Constrained Aspect Ratio, and make sure that the width and height fields are set to 1 as shown above. This will constrain the tool to making perfectly round circular selections.

10. Use the Circular Marquee to select an area on one side of the button (the size of the circular selection will determine the size of the LED); once you're happy with the results, save the selection into a new alpha channel.

11. Make the RGB channels active, by clicking on RGB in the Channels palette. Load the LED mask as a selection by dragging it over the Make Selection icon at the bottom of the Channels palette.

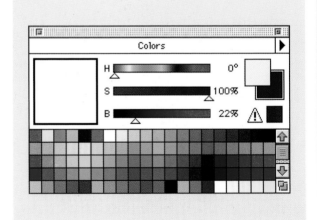

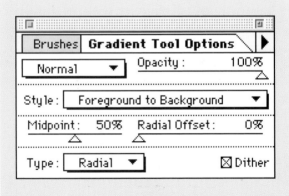

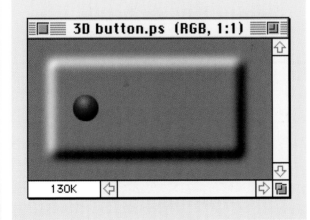

12. For this example, the LED will be red, so we'll make the foreground color a light red and the background color a dark maroon. This technique works equally well with any base color. ▲ *Use the Colors floating palette, choose HSB as the color selection mode. This makes it easy to choose red as the base hue, and dial up brightness variations with the Brightness slider.*

13. Double click on the Gradient tool, and set the type to Radial. Position the cursor inside of the loaded selection from the previous step (in the upper part of the selection), and drag the cursor to the edge of the loaded selection.

You should end up with results looking like the above example. Of course, you can change the direction of the gradient to change the position of the light reflecting on the LED.

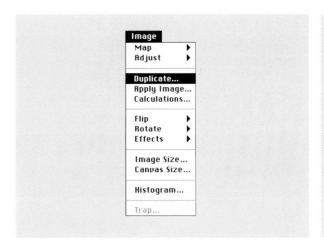

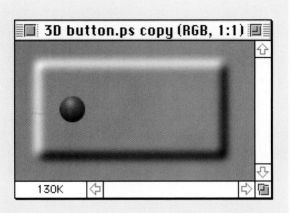

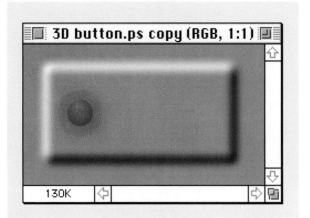

14. Time to make a lit version of the button. Choose Duplicate from the Image menu. This will make a duplicate of the image with all of its channels, paths and layers.

The duplicate file will open with the same title with the word copy attached to it.

15. Load the LED alpha channel. Choose the Feather command from the Select menu, and enter a value of 10 (the larger the feather, the softer the resulting glow effect). In the Color palette, choose a bright red for the foreground color, and fill the feathered selection with the red (for this example, we filled 2 times to beef up the brightness and density of the red colorization). Result: a glowing LED.

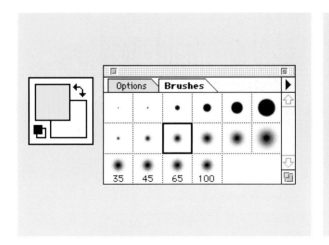

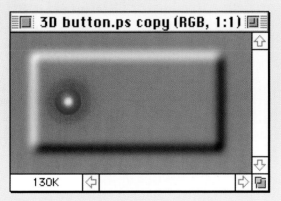

16. Next a light source within the LED is created. A bright yellow is chosen for the Foreground color and an Airbrush with soft edges.

17. A small dot is applied to the center of the LED. The LED is now lit.

18. All you have to do now is convert the two button images to indexed color (we prefer an 8-bit, System palette with diffusion dither for most of our own work). Save to disk or copy to clipboard. Import the two images into an animation program. You now have a two-stage button which lights up with a fairly realistic glow. Place and animate to taste.

32

Glory Shot

In this exercise, you will create a "glory shot" for a product that does not yet exist. A "glory shot" is an image which calls attention to a product or package of a product for advertising or promotional material. The product being highlighted in this exercise is a book.

1. To follow along you can create an image like the one shown above or scan the cover and spine of an existing book.

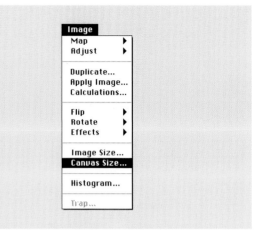

Increasing the canvas size

2. Increase the canvas size to allow enough space to display two copies of the cover stacked vertically. A little space on the sides is also advisable. To increase the canvas size you choose Canvas Size from the Image menu.

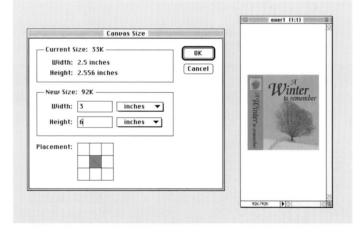

The dialog box shows the current dimensions of the image. Entering new measurements will apply them to the canvas. The box at the bottom allows you to choose the position of the current image within the expanded canvas.

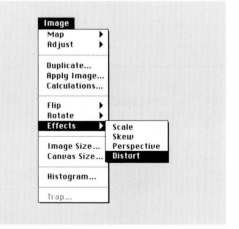

Distorting the image

3. Select the front cover portion of the image with the Rectangle selection tool. Choose the Distort tool from the Effects sub menu of the Image menu.

4. Grab and move the points on the right to create the illusion of perspective as in the sample shown. Deselect.

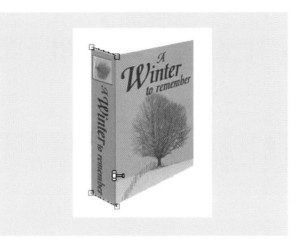

5. Select the spine portion of the book cover and, as before, distort it in the opposite direction of the cover, thus giving the illusion of a box in perspective. DO NOT DESELECT.

Adding depth

6. With a small Airbrush with the Opacity set to 40% and Black as the Foreground color, spray a slight tone along the outside edge of the spine to add a little dimension. Deselect.

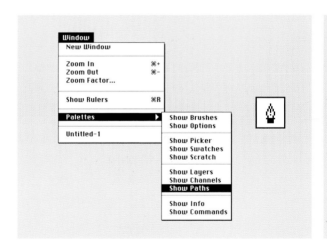

7. Go to the Windows menu and down to the Palettes sub menu and choose Show Paths. In the window, choose the Path tool.

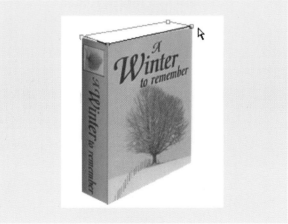

8. Click four points above the box to form the top of box.

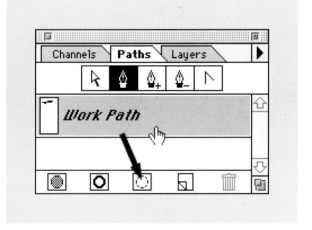

9. In the Path tool window click and drag the Work path down to the Make Selection icon at the bottom of the window to make it a selection.

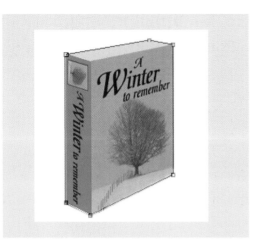

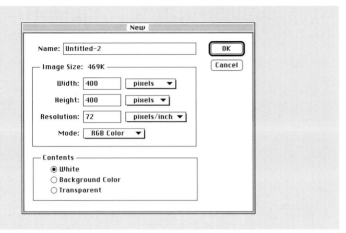

10. Select a medium gray for the Foreground color. Press Option and Delete to fill the selected area with 100% of the foreground color.

11. The box is now complete. With the Path tool, select the entire image of the box. Make it a selection as before and press Command-C to copy it to the clipboard.

12. Press Command-N or select New from the File menu to start a new file. Make it 400 pixels square, and choose 72 for resolution (make sure the settings are in pixels). These numbers are for this exercise. If this was a real assignment, the dimensions and resolution would be determined by the requirements of the actual project.

13. Press Command-I or choose Invert from the Map sub menu of the Image menu. This turns your background black.

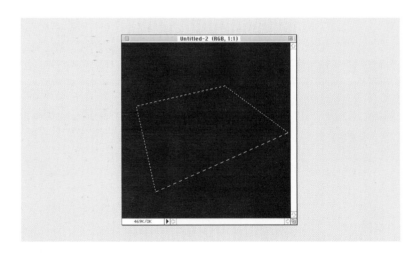

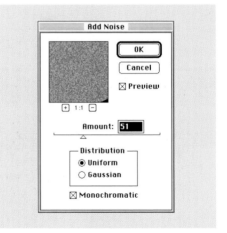

Creating a 3-dimensional stone plate
14. With the Lasso and the Option key pressed *This turns the Lasso into rubber band or straight line mode,* select a shape to be the plate on which the book will stand. Choose a medium gray for the Foreground color. Press Option-Delete to fill the selection with the gray. Save the file and name it whatever you wish.

Adding texture
15. Choose Add Noise from the Filters menu.

In the dialog box, move the slider to about 51. Make sure to click on the Monochromatic button.

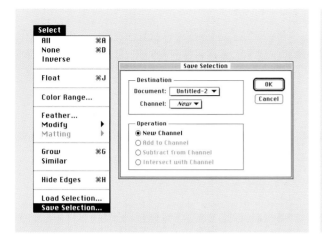

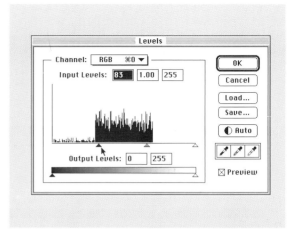

Creating an Alpha channel

16. Now you must create an Alpha channel for the plate. Choose Save Selection from the Select menu. Press OK in the dialog box that pops up.

17. Press Command-0 (zero) to return to the RGB composite.

Adding depth

18. With the Lasso tool and the Option button pressed, select the left edge of the plate.

19. Choose the Levels control found under Adjust in the Image menu. To darken the edge, move the left triangle, which is black and controls the dark tones of the image, to the right.

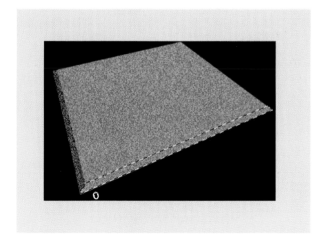

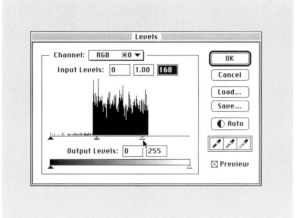

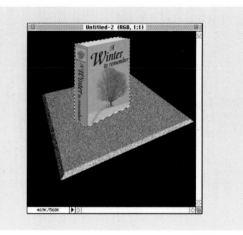

20. Select the front edge of the plate.

21. Choose the Levels control again, found under Adjust in the Image menu. This time to lighten the front edge, move the rightmost triangle, which is white and controls the light tones of the image, to the left.

22. Press Command-V to paste the contents of the clipboard (the book) onto the plate. Position it where you want it then choose Save Selection from the Select menu to create an alpha channel of it.

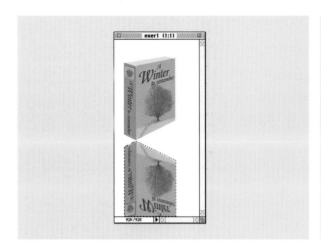

Creating a reflection

23. Go to the original box file (Winter Book). Paste a copy of the box and position it below the original. DO NOT DESELECT. Choose Flip Vertical from the Image menu.

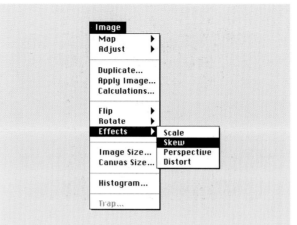

24. Deselect.

25. With the Lasso selection tool and the Option button pressed, select the front of the book.

26. Choose the Skew option under Effects in the Image menu.

27. Move the handles to skew the art to line up with the original book.

28. Do the same for the spine of the book. This will serve as the reflection on the stone plate. Select the entire reflection with the Path tool and copy it to the clipboard. Go to the file with the plate.

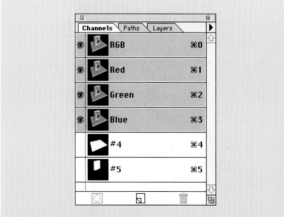

Creating a special alpha channel

The reflection needs to fade off to get a realistic effect. You must now create an alpha channel through which you will paste the reflection. You have the original alpha channels of the plate and the book.

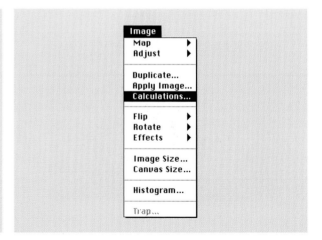

29. Choose Calculations from the Image menu.

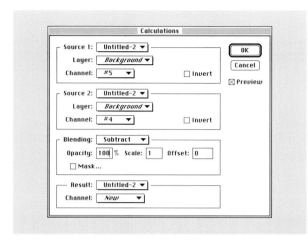

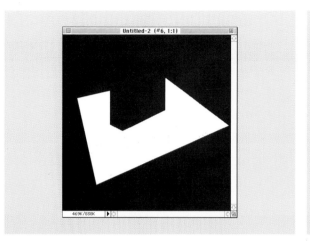

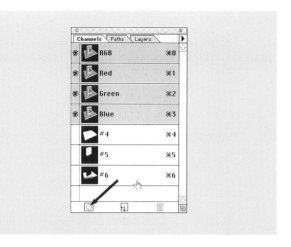

30. In the dialog box that pops up, make Channel #5 Source 1. Channel #4 should be Source 2. Set Blending to Subtract with an Opacity of 100%. The Result is set to a New Channel in the same file.

This will create a new channel which will expose the plate while protecting the book.

31. In the new channel, load it as a selection onto itself by clicking and dragging the icon of it in the Channels window over to the Make Selection icon at the bottom of the window.

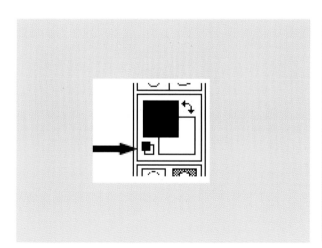

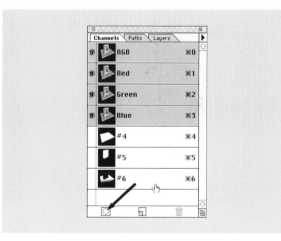

32. Return the foreground and background colors to the default black and white by clicking the small icon in the Tools palette.

33. With the Blend tool, create a blend with black at the bottom, working upward to white by the bottom of the book. Deselect.

34. Press Command-0 (zero) to return to the RGB image. Load that final alpha channel by dragging it over the Make Selection icon.

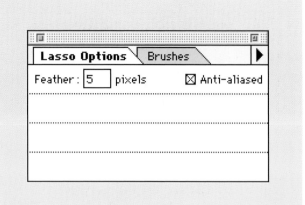

35. Choose Paste Into from the Edit menu. Position the reflection under the box. DO NOT DESELECT.

36. Bring down the Opacity by pressing the number keys on the keyboard (i.e. 5=50%, 8=80% etc.). Deselect.

Relection of light source

37. To create a glare from some imaginary light source across the plate, choose the Lasso tool and set Feather to about 5.

With the Lasso and the Option button pressed, to get a straight line selection, select an area across the plate as shown above.

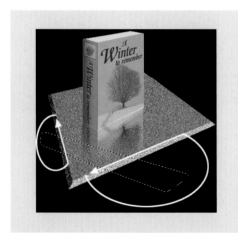
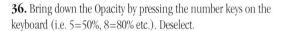

38. With the Lasso reset to zero, deselect the area along the edges by surrounding the outside selected areas. The reason for this is to have the selection soft within the plate but sharp at the edges.

Lighten the area with the Levels command under Adjust in the Image menu.

39. Select an area behind the box and darken it with the Levels command.

Creating a spotlight

40. With the Elliptical selection tool, select a circle on the front of the box.

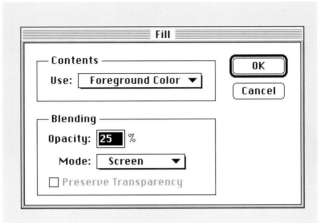

41. With the Lasso, the Option and Shift keys pressed, select a cone shape as shown.

42. Make the foreground color white.

43. Choose Fill under the Edit menu. Fill the selection with 25% of the foreground color with the Mode set to Screen.

The result should look like this.

44. With the Elliptical selection tool, once again, select a circle on the front of the box. Choose Feather from the Select menu and enter 4 for the amount.

45. With the Rectangular Selection tool and the Command key pressed, deselect the side edges. It will appear as if the front of the box is lit.

46. Lighten the area with the Levels control under Adjust in the Image Menu. Deselect. Voila! You are done.

33

Painting

Photoshop is thought of primarily as an image manipulation program. Basically that is considered photo retouching. Photoshop is also, however, a powerful paint program.

The image above is called "bean bins." It was created entirely with the computer using Adobe Illustrator and Adobe Photoshop, without the use of scans. Here, we will show how parts of the image were created.

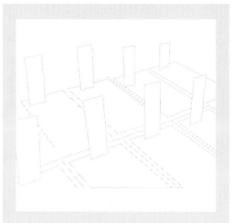

The basic shape was outlined using the basic tools in Illustrator and then imported into Photoshop. The outline is then used as a guide into which color and texture will be added. This process is similar to traditional painting in which a sketch is first drawn on the canvas with a pencil or charcoal, over which the paint is added.

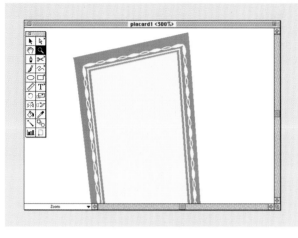

Each element is first created in Illustrator because of its ease of use for such things as the pattern along the edge of the placards. The Illustrator files are saved in their own format (Illustrator).

In Photoshop, using the Place command under the File menu, the elements are imported.

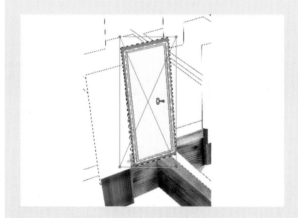

The elements come in and are moved into position. Using the Airbrush tool, highlights and cracks are added.

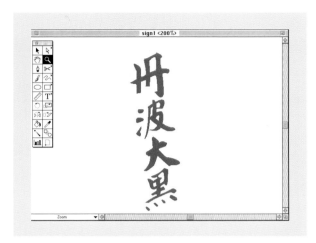

The lettering on the placard is done separately in Illustrator since its texture will be different.

It is placed into the Photoshop image.

As with the placard, highlights and texture are added to give the illusion that they were lettered by hand.

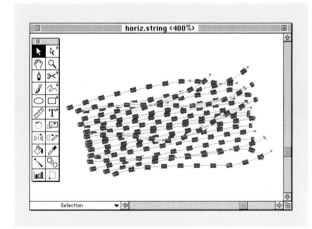

The string ties, visible in the lower left corner of the image, were created in Illustrator using a simple technique. Lines were drawn and given a white stroke of a desired thickness. They were then copied to the clipboard. Paste in Front was used to paste a copy directly over the original white lines. These new lines were given a blue stroke which was then dashed.

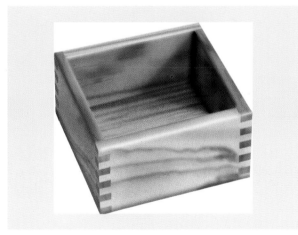

The wood textures were created in Photoshop.

Areas to be worked on were segregated via alpha channels. This allows easy selection for various techniques.

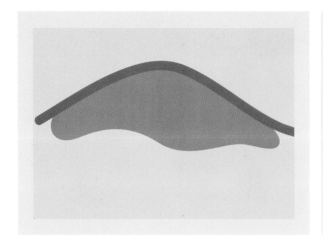

Each area is filled with a basic color. With the Airbrush tool, details like grain and nicks are added. The grain is achieved with a dark, thin line which serves as the grain itself. Below it a softer, lighter tone is added to serve as the sweep that appears in wood grains.

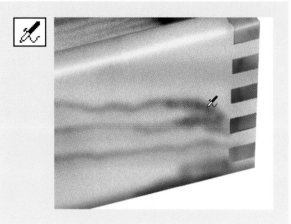

In the end, the shapes will be blurred and the Add Noise filter will be applied to add texture.

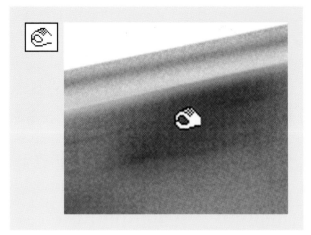

The edge where the two meet is softened with the Blur tool. With the Burn tool, areas are darkened.

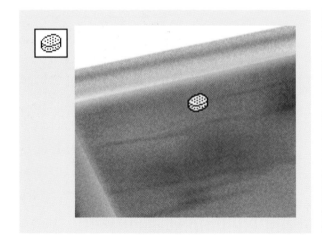

Areas are discolored to simulate wear and age. The Desaturate tool is used to accomplish this effect.

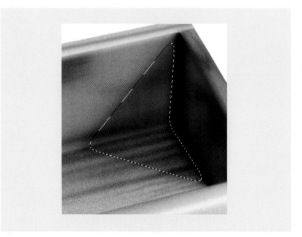

With a Feathered Lasso (the Feather can be entered in the Lasso Options palette), the areas which fall into shadow are selected and filled with a translucent black or darkened using the Levels command.

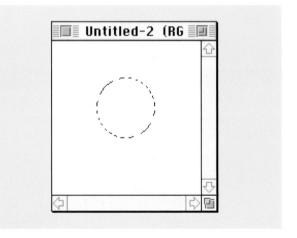

Creating the beans
The beans started out as selections.

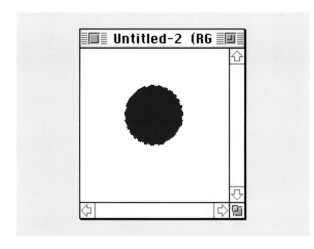

The selection gets filled with the desired color.

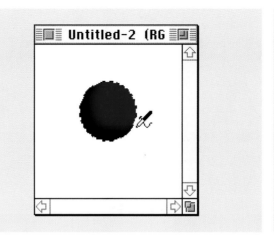

Using the Airbrush tool, a shadow is added for dimensionality.

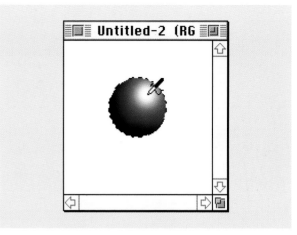

With a lighter shade of the bean color, a highlight is added.

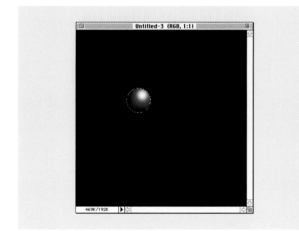

The bean is then copied over to a new file where the background is set to black. The bean is placed into its own layer.

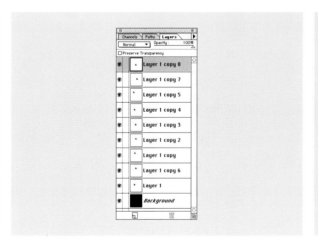

The layer is duplicated many times to create a multitude of beans.

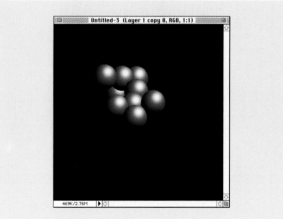

Each layer is moved to form a cluster of beans.

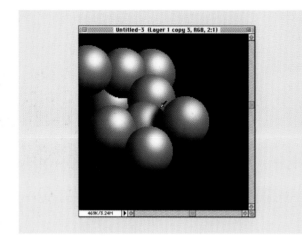

Where appropriate, a shadow is added to give depth and realism to the cluster of beans.

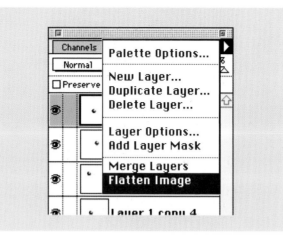

The layers are Flattened to the background to form a single image.

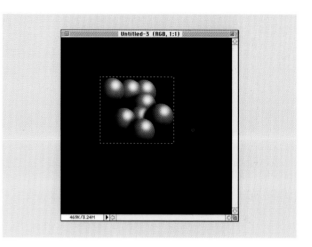

The cluster is then selected.

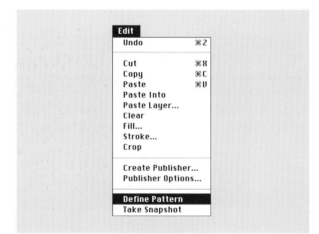

Define Pattern is chosen from the Edit menu.

Fill is chosen from the Edit menu.

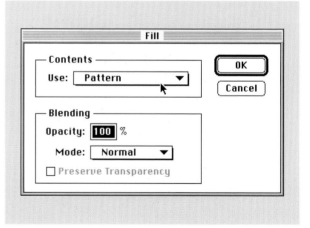

Pattern is selected for the Use.

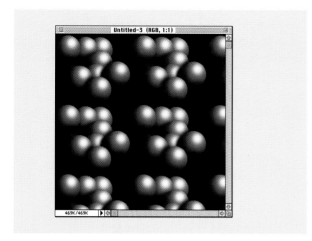  

The pattern of the bean clusters fills the canvas.

The original bean is pasted over the pattern.

Additional beans are copied over the pattern to breakup the pattern. Additional shadows are painted over the pattern to accommodate the new beans.

The same technique is used for the various types of beans. The final result is a realistic image of a bean market.

Formats

Photoshop 3.0

Photoshop recognizes a variety of formats and allows you to save images to the same variety of formats. It is important to understand what the different formats represent and when to use which.

It is best to work in the native Photoshop 3.0 format. This format has 24-bit color information and one of the best lossless compression ratios when saving. The native Photoshop 3.0 format stores all the paths, layers and alpha channels for later use. This format opens and saves much faster and is the most memory efficient.

When you have layers incorporated into the file, Photoshop 3.0 is the only format available when you do a Save As. Earlier versions of Photoshop would warn you upon saving to another format that image data, such as extra alpha channels, would be lost. In Photoshop 3.0, a format that does not support layers or a certain number of alpha channels will not be available as an option in the Save As dialog box. When you have the maximum number of channels (24) used, Photoshop 3.0, Raw and TIFF are the only file formats available.

If your image has 16 or fewer channels, the Photoshop 2.0 format becomes available. This format recognizes a total of 16 channels; for example, an RGB image with up to 13 alpha channels, or a CMYK image with up to 12 channels, could be saved in this format.

When an image has but one alpha channel, the formats PICT, PICT Resource, PIXAR and Targa become active. These formats support an image's color channels plus one alpha channel.

A CMYK image file can be saved as Photoshop 3.0, Photoshop 2.0, EPS, JPEG, Raw, ScitexCT or TIFF. They do not save alpha channels or layers.

Indexed Color images can be saved as Photoshop 3.0, Photoshop 2.0, Amiga IFF, BMP, CompuServe GIF, PCX, PICT, PICT Resource, PixelPaint, Raw, Targa or TIFF.

8-bit Grayscale images can be saved as Photoshop 3.0, Photoshop 2.0, Amiga IFF, BMP, CompuServe GIF, EPS, JPEG, PCX, PICT, PICT Resource, PIXAR, PixelPaint, Raw, ScitexCT, Targa and TIFF.

1-bit Bitmap images can be saved as Photoshop 3.0, Photoshop 2.0, Amiga IFF, BMP, CompuServe GIF, EPS, MacPaint, PCX, PICT, PICT Resource, PixelPaint and TIFF.

Photoshop 2.0

This is the native format for earlier versions of Photoshop. Photoshop 2.5, the version released before 3.0, is not an option for saving. Photoshop 3.0 will open 2.5 documents. This format is good for delivering files to clients whose use of Photoshop might be limited, and who might not have the 3.0 upgrade.

Amiga IFF

The Amiga Interchange File Format is a standard for paint programs on the Amiga platform. The color bit depth can be from 1 bit (black & white) to 8 bits (256 colors).

BMP

This is the format which is common to IBM PC-compatible computers. The color bit depth can be from 1 bit (black & white) to 8 bits (256 colors). You are given the option to save to Microsoft Windows or the OS/2® operating systems.

CompuServe GIF

GIF, or Graphic Interchange Format, is useful for saving and opening files to or from the CompuServe telecommunications network. This format encodes the image as an alphanumeric file for uploading and downloading for LZW compression and cross-platform translation. GIF is an 8-bit format.

The GIF format is rapidly becoming one of the favored file formats for displaying graphics on the World Wide Web portion of the Internet (these Web pages are created in HTML, which stands for Hyper Text Markup Language), due to a feature called interleaving. By interleaving a GIF file, Web browsers can build the image's resolution gradually, rather than holding up all browsing functions while downloading a non-interleaved image file (GIF files can also be created in non-interleaved format). GIF files can also have a single color defined as transparent, for compositing and placement in Web pages or layout programs. Unfortunately, Photoshop doesn't support either of these important options when saving GIF (only non-interleaved format is provided).

EPS

The EPS (Encapsulated PostScript) format is a "resolution independent" file format, meaning that the output of the file will default to the output device's highest possible resolution, rather than being dependent on the pixel-per-inch resolution of the file itself. It is the best format for transferring files to a page layout or drawing/illustration program. If you plan to incorporate your image into an Adobe Illustrator document (as an element, not a template), this is the only format to save it in. The file will contain the PostScript information for printing as well as a PICT preview for placement viewing within the layout program. The color depth of the PICT preview has no bearing on how the image will print.

If the image is Grayscale then it is best to keep it as a TIFF since the EPS file will be considerably larger. If, however, you have assigned halftone or transfer function information to the document you must save it as EPS for that information to be transferred.

Filmstrip

Filmstrip is a format utilized by Adobe Premiere, a QuickTime video editing program. Video clips saved as Filmstrip from within Premiere come into Photoshop as a single file, literally a strip of the clip's frames and their corresponding time code attached. The clip can then be modified in Photoshop, making the format very useful for exacting special effects and

rotoscoping work. Opening the modified Filmstrip in Premiere will return it to a video clip. The important thing to remember here is that the Filmstrip, when imported into Photoshop, might have extra channels (besides the RGB channels) — it's crucial not to remove or delete these extra channels, as they are required to save the Filmstrip back out again.

JPEG

The JPEG (Joint Photographic Experts Group) format is a "lossy" compression system, which means it discards image data in order to maximize storage needs. JPEG describes an image by allocating color values to ranges of pixels (specified as arrays), rather than specifying a color value separately to each pixel. This process is accomplished through the use of a mathematical process called DCT (Discrete Cosine Transforms). This drastically reduces the amount of storage the image requires, at the expense of significantly reduced image quality and detail (The amount of compression is definable for each image file). The format was primarily designed to remove information from an image meant to be transferred over standard telephone lines and reproduced with a screening process (which inherently reduces image detail found in the source digital data file). The native bit depth of the format is 24 bit.

Extreme amounts of JPEG compression will result in a visible degradation of the image's quality, creating bands of discoloration or splotchy areas of color. Despite these

limitations, however, it remains a very popular means of compressing images for transferal over computer networks. Compression and decompression are slow, and best assisted by the use of specialized hardware boards with JPEG encoding/decoding chips.

MacPaint

MacPaint was the first graphics application on the Mac. It is limited to an 8.5 x 11-inch portrait letter size. It is also limited to 1 bit of color (black & white). The MacPaint format is only available when an image has had its mode set to Bitmap.

PCX

This is a format developed by Zsoft for its PC-based Paintbrush software. It originally saved only 16 colors, but recent updates accommodate 8-bit and 16-bit color.

PICT

PICT was designed for moving images into other paint programs or multimedia applications. PICT integrates seamlessly into hundreds of applications, Apple's QuickDraw, and the Macintosh clipboard. PICT images can have several color depth settings—anywhere from 1 bit per pixel (black & white) to 32 bits per pixel (full 24-bit color with a single 8-bit alpha channel).

PICT Resource

This is the format used to create custom startup screens and for creating PICT resources for inclusion in an application. This is of use to programmers creating software applications. You may be asked to save to this format if you are commissioned to create images to be part of a program.

PIXAR

This is the format used to transfer images to the high-end PIXAR workstation. These workstations are in wide use primarily in the film industry for the production of special effects. The format is 24 bit, with a single alpha channel.

PixelPaint

PixelPaint is a paint program available on the Macintosh platform. PixelPaint also accepts PICT; this format is largely a remnant of earlier versions.

Raw

The Raw format is a generic raster format, primarily used for transporting images to other types of computers. Using the Raw format, however, requires exact knowledge of the data contained in the image to accurately translate it into Photoshop.

Scitex CT

Images can be saved in Scitex CT format from either the grayscale or CMYK modes. This format allows you to transport an image to a Scitex workstation for high-end color separations and incorporation into page layouts. The native color space of the Scitex CT format is CMYK.

Targa

In the IBM PC world, the Targa format is the standard for graphics and paint box programs built to utilize the True Vision Targa and Vista video boards.

TIFF

TIFF (Tagged-Image File Format) is one of the more useful formats for transporting color and grayscale images into page-layout programs. TIFF is essentially a variable-resolution raster/bitmap file.

TIFF files have a compression option called LZW, which sometimes creates a slight softening of the image. It is wise to use caution with this compression feature, as not all page-layout programs read or generate LZW TIFF files.

Glossary

A

additive primary colors Red, green and blue, combinations of which are used to create all other colors when direct or transmitted light is used. They are called additive because when all three are superimposed on each other the resulting color is white.

address The exact location in computer memory where a particular piece of data is stored.

algorithm A set of instructions for solving a computer problem by setting up a series of step-by-step programming commands. An algorithm is independent of the language being used to program.

alpha channel An 8-bit, grayscale channel used for masking techniques.

alphanumeric Computer data which is made up of numbers and letters.

analog An electronic signal consisting of varying voltage levels. The quality of analog signals is much lower than digital signals and suffers from degradation when duplicated.

animatic A rough representation of an animation. Used for storyboarding animation sequences.

animation The process of creating the illusion of movement. By creating incremental changes in position, form, color, etc. between frames.

anti-aliasing The process of blending the color of adjacent pixels to eliminate the "jaggies" or stair-stepping associated with pixel-based images.

application A computer program.

arbitrary map The pencil function in the Curves dialog box. By changing the shape of the curves with the pencil tool, you can very specifically control brightness and density values along any part of the spectrum of the image. It's also used to control the amount of black in a color separation.

architecture The overall structure of computer software and hardware in terms of how they interact.

ASCII Acronym for American Standard Code for Information Interchange. It assigns a unique binary number to each character and control character.

aspect ratio The ratio of height to width.

attribute Computer term which relates to characteristics of an image such as its color and size. In word processing or page layout programs, it denotes the size, font and style of characters.

axis The imaginary line around which an object rotates.

B

background color The color which represents the canvas when using the Eraser tool. Also the ending color when creating blends or gradients.

bézier curve A path that relies on a series of mathematical curve definitions. Named after Pierre Bézier.

bicubic An interpolation method used to generate intermediate pixels (during operations such as resize and arbitrary rotate) which yields highest quality at the expense of increased processing time.

bilinear An interpolation method used to generate intermediate pixels (during operations such as resize and arbitrary rotate) which combines relatively high quality with faster processing times.

binary The numbering system which is based on the concept of a memory location, or bit, being either on or off.

bit Abbreviation for Binary Digit. The basic unit of information which is the foundation of all computing.

bit depth The amount of information contained in a single pixel.

bitmap In computer graphics, it refers to an image made up of pixels, each having a specific size (which is expressed in terms of resolution), distinct color and brightness value. In Photoshop it specifically refers to an image having a single channel with 1-bit of information per pixel in which all colors are represented by either black or white.

black generation The amount of black density in the black plate of a separated CMYK file.

black ink limit The maximum amount of total ink coverage that a specific printing process (or press) can accurately handle.

bluescreen A process used to isolate foreground images from a pure blue background (devoid of any red or green values).

Bluescreen extraction and compositing is used to facilitate the creation of masks, especially for objects with complex edge characteristics (such as hair).

blur The process of reducing contrast between adjacent pixels to deliver the perception of smoother intermediate tones and increased image softness.

brightness One of the three attributes of color; hue and saturation are the other two. It is a term used to describe the intensity of light.

buffer Temporary storage area in a computer or output device used to store data until it is required for processing.

bug A defect in computer software or hardware. The term came from an insect which wandered into the circuitry of the vacuum tube of the first electronic hardware and caused a short-circuit.

bull's-eyes Marks that appear on the individual films of a separation used for alignment.

bump map In 3D graphics, the technique of adding surface roughness or bumpiness to an object without actually changing or affecting the geometry of the shape; the effect is seen only when the image is rendered.

burn The process of overexposing an image, which makes it lighter.

C

calculations Photoshop operations which compare the pixels of two images and apply discrete logic testing to yield a resulting set of pixels.

calibration The process of equalizing and balancing the color values of different steps of a production process, including scanning, display and output devices.

calibration bars A set of swatches on the side of a printed image to denote the 11-step grayscale on the black plate.

canvas size The dimensions of a file.

caption Descriptive text that appears below an image on a printed page.

CCD Charged Coupled Device. A light-sensitive electronic chip used as a temporary image storage device in scanners and video cameras. When light hits a CCD, the color and brightness information is converted to digital information which the computer understands.

CD-ROM Compact Disc-Read Only Memory. A type of optical disc used to store large quantities of data. The information is stored in a series of plateaus and valleys. When a laser light bounces off these plateaus it is converted into binary code.

channel The discrete components of an image. The colors Red, Green and Blue, each reside in their own channel. Images saved in Photoshop can have up to 24 channels. Besides brightness and color information, additional document channels are used for masking.

characteristic curve A plotted curve which demonstrates the change in density of an image as the exposure is increased. The slope of this curve is the measure of gamma, or contrast.

clipping groups The technique of "grouping" multiple layers together which uses the bottom-most layer as an 8-bit mask for all other layers grouped with it.

clipping paths Vector-based selection masks which can be imbedded into an EPS image for silhouetting bitmap images

with resolution-independent masks in external programs such as Illustrator, PageMaker and Quark XPress.

cloning The process of copying portions of an image into other areas of an image.

CMYK Cyan, Magenta, Yellow and Black, which are the four process colors in printing.

CMYK image An image made up of four channels. Each channel contains the information for the individual process colors Cyan, Magenta, Yellow and Black.

chroma The intensity of color in an image.

color correction The process of manipulating the color information of an image to optimize the printing process.

color depth The number of colors available to each pixel. The information is stored in bits. The greater the number of bits, the greater the selection of color. 8-bit = 256 colors 24-bit = 16.8 million colors.

color difference matte Any of the matting processes which use the color of the image as a base for separating the image from the background. Any color can be used provided the image is devoid of that color. Bluescreen and Greenscreen are color difference mattes.

color lookup table (CLUT) A special palette that stores the colors used in an image.

color map A table of information used by the computer to adjust the color and brightness of an image.

color separation An image which has been broken down into the four process colors of cyan, magenta, yellow and black. Each channel contains the individual color information which is translated onto plates used in the printing process.

comp In the graphic design industry, it stands for a rough representation of a finished product used for client presentations and such. In imaging, it is an abbreviation of composite.

composite The result of taking two or more images and combining them to form one image.

constrain To restrict the movement of a tool or the proportions of a selection tool or image.

continuous-tone image An image containing gradient tones.

contrast The relative difference, or "spread" between the dark and light values of an image.

crop To select a portion of an image and delete the unselected areas.

crop marks Marks printed with an image to indicate the outer edges where the image will be trimmed.

D

data Information which is stored, transmitted or manipulated in a computer or electronic device.

database An organized collection of data capable of being searched or cross-referenced easily.

DCS Desktop Color Separation, the file format used to export pre-separated CMYK images in EPS format for inclusion in full-color pages in PageMaker or Quark XPress. DCS produces five files—four for the CMYK plates, and a screen file for placement in the page layout.

debugging The process of identifying and correcting errors (bugs) in computer hardware or software.

defloat The process of anchoring a floating selection.

defringe The process of removing the edge artifacts created when an object is isolated from a background and placed (composited) into a new background with different color or brightness values. The anti-aliased pixels from the first background are removed, and the edges are mixed with the colors in the new background, to create a more seamless edge.

degradation The loss of quality of an image when duplicated or manipulated.

densitometer An instrument used to measure the density of printed halftones by taking readings from the calibration bars. Also an instrument for measuring the opacity of a film image. This reading plays an important part in the determination of proper bluescreen exposure and matte density.

density The opacity of a film image. An opaque image which transmits no light has the maximum density, while a totally transparent one has no density.

density range In printing, the range from the smallest dot (highlight) to the largest dot (shadow) a press can handle.

depth of field The range of focus in front and behind the principal subject of an image.

desaturation The loss of color intensity.

difference matte The mask created when applying difference matting techniques.

difference matting The process of separating elements of an image by comparing the difference in color values between them. The foreground elements are separated from the background by calculating the difference between the background and the image pixel values.

digital Format of information which is converted and stored as numerical sequences of ones and zeros which are deciphered by a computer. Any device or process which manipulates digital information.

digitize The process of converting 2D or 3D static or dynamic visual or audio forms into binary information.

digitizing pen Also called a stylus, is an electronic pen used in conjunction with a digitizing tablet to control the position of a cursor on the screen.

digitizing table/tablet A drawing pad which is relative to the computer screen. Passing a digitizing pen over the pad will move the position of the cursor.

dithering The process of creating patterns of colors to simulate colors absent in an image or unavailable for display. Examples include the patterns of black and white pixels in a bitmap image to simulate grayscale values and the screen patterns created when viewing a high-quality image on a low-quality computer display.

D-1 format A high-quality digital videotape format. Comparable, in film, to the negative.

displacement map One image whose pixel values are used to distort another image. Lower pixel (darker) values result in less distortion, while higher pixel (lighter) values distort the image more.

displacement mapping The process of distorting an image to form a surface texture.

dodge The limiting of exposure of an image to cause it to appear darker.

duotone An image printed with only two standard, often Pantone, ink colors.

download The process of transfering data from one computer to another. Usually refers to transferring data from an on-line network to an individual computer.

dot gain A defect in printing causing dots to print larger than intended. Often caused by the ink absorbency of a particular paper.

DPI Dots per inch; a measure of resolution. The number of dots that a printer will produce within an inch. The higher the number, the more detail will be visible.

dubbing The process of duplicating data onto different media, be it computer storage media or audio/video tape.

dupe Short for duplication. A duplicate of the original. The process of making a duplication.

dynamic range The range of colors and values a computer is able to represent based on the number of bits which are used to record each color. The higher the number of bits, the higher the dynamic range.

E

edge characteristics The appearance of the edge of an element which has been composited into another image.

eight bit color The color depth of an image which has 8 bits of information per pixel. Eight bits allows for each pixel to contain one of 256 colors.

eight bit monitor The amount of color a monitor can display. This has no bearing on the image itself.

element A single image which is being composited into another.

EPS Encapsulated PostScript; graphics format for bringing images into object-based drawing and page layout programs. It

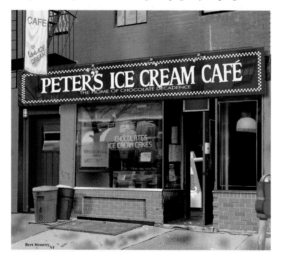

is resolution-independent, meaning the output resolution is based on the output device, not the image file. Besides the image description data, an EPS file also carries a preview PICT or TIFF file, used in displaying the image on the screen.

exabyte A tape storage medium which is capable of storing 2.2 gigabytes of information.

export A file is exported when another version of it is needed in another file format or for a specific purpose, such as output.

external memory Any memory storage device conected to a computer to augment its internal storage hard disk.

F

fade-out rate The rate at which the Paintbrush or Airbrush tool runs out of paint to simulate a real brush stroke.

feather Gradually fades out the edges of a brush or selection, giving variably soft edges.

fill To paint a selected area with a color or pattern.

fixed hard disk Any disk drive which is permanently attached to a computer.

flare A visual effect to simulate a bright light source being distorted and accentuated as if seen through a real optical lens.

flatten Taking an image with layers and merging the layers into a single background layer.

flip The process of making a mirror image of the original or reversing the facing of a selection or image.

foreground color The color used by all the tools which utilize a color (Paintbrush, Pencil, Line tool, etc.)

floating selection A selection which has been floated,

moved or copied over an image. It can be modified independently of the pixels of the underlying image. It will not become part of the underlying image until it is deselected.

fractal A visual algorithm that when repeated forms a greater image of essentially the same character.

frame grab The process of digitizing a single frame of video into a digital image file.

frame grabber A device for making frame grabs.

fuzziness A means of controlling the amount of anti-aliasing which will be applied to the edges of a selection. Similar to feathering.

G

gamma The objective measurement of contrast in an image.

gamma curve See characteristic curve.

generation The reference given to the number of copies made of an original. In film or analog duplication this is an

important factor which will determine the level of degradation.

gamut The range of colors a given color system can visually represent.

generation loss The loss of quality of an image due to duplication.

gigabyte One thousand megabytes or one billion bytes.

grain A noise texture which appears on film images. This is due to the silver halide particles which make up film emulsion. The grain is microscopic but becomes visible when an image is enlarged. The grain increases with each generation of reproduction.

gradient fill A fill method which consists of the gradual transition of multiple colors.

grayscale image A single channel image which consists of 256 levels of gray.

gray-component replacement (GCR) The removal of CMYK and replacing their values with values of black.

gray ramp A graph representing the density of equal amounts of neutral colors (equal amounts of cyan, magenta, and yellow) in an image. Used in color separation.

H

halftone The reproduction of a continuous-tone image made by using a screen to break up the image into dots of varying sizes. The proximity and location of these dots on the printed page gives the illusion of continuous colors.

handles The extension of the points made by the Path tool which allow for the manipulation of the beziér curve between two points.

hard copy Images viewed in printed form rather than on the monitor.

hard disk A metal disk coated with magnetic material used to store computer data.

highlight The lightest parts of an image. In a halftone, this area is represented by the smallest dots or the absence of dots.

histogram A graphic representation of the number of pixels with a given color value. It shows the breakdown of the tone gamut and color occurrence in an image.

hot An area of an image which is too bright.

hue The main attribute of a color which distinguishes it from another color.

I

icon A picture or symbol used to represent a tool, command, etc., in a computer.

image enhancement To improve the quality of an image by reducing noise, increasing contrast, etc.

image mapping The process of placing an image over a three-dimensional shape in 3D programs.

imagesetter An output device for plate ready art.

indexed color A single channel image with 8 bits of color per pixel. Unlike a grayscale image, it contains color rather than levels of gray. The index is a color lookup table which contains 256 colors.

interactive The process of providing real time response or feedback to the user.

interpolation A mathematical operation that averages nearby pixel values together; used when resizing an image or selection.

intermediate negative The reversal print of an original negative from which prints can be made without risking damage to the original.

intermediate positive A positive made from an original negative used for compositing purposes.

interneg Short for intermediate negative.

interpos Short for intermediate positive.

J

jaggies Stair-stepping caused by pixels on the edge of the elements of an image.

JPEG A lossy compression system used to compress color images. JPEG stands for Joint Photographic Experts Group.

K

kern To adjust the space between characters in type.

keyword A word given as a database search parameter.

L

lab color A color model that interprets color as one lightness component, ranging from black to white, and two color components, the first ranging from green to red, the second ranging from blue to yellow. This is the native color space for PostScript Level 2.

laser disk See optical disk.

laser printer An output device which uses lasers to set ink onto paper.

layer A component of object-based raster imaging, wherein a set of pixels can be separately addressable from the rest of the pixels in the image. Photoshop can have up to 100 layers, including the background.

layer mask An 8-bit grayscale component of a layer that determines its opacity.

leading The space between lines of text.

light value The degree of brightness or darkness in an image.

linear fill A fill which is projected from one point to another in a straight line.

low res Short for low resolution, an image which has insufficient information for final reproduction. Low res images are used for presentation of work in progress or can be set to the monitor resolution and used for on-screen presentations.

lpi Lines per inch, refers to how many halftone screen lines can be measured within a linear inch.

luminance The highest of the individual RGB values plus the lowest of the individual RGB values, divided by two.

luminosity A color parameter that measures the brightness of color.

LZW compression An image compression scheme used with the TIFF file format.

M

marching ants The term used to descibe the animated lines which indicate a selected area of an image.

marquee The area of a selection is outlined by a series of traveling dashes (marching ants).

mask An area used to protect a portion of an image while exposing others for manipulation. Often based on an 8-bit grayscale component that varies the mask's opacity based on levels of brightness, black being opaque and white being transparent.

matte The portion of a mask which protects the image from manipulation.

meg Short for megabyte (one million bytes).

menu A list displayed on the computer screen of commands available to the user.

menu bar A strip along the top of the computer screen which contains the menu items.

midtone A range of tones whose value is approximately halfway between the lightest and darkest value of an image.

modem Contraction for Modulator-Demodulator. A device which enables the transfer of computer data over phone lines.

moiré pattern An undesirable pattern in printing caused by incorrect angles set to overlying halftones.

monotone An image printed with only one non-black ink.

morph The process of progressively transforming one object into another. The name derives from metamorphosis, and usually is a hybrid process of cross-fading and distorting.

morphing The process of creating a morph.

multichannel image An image consisting of more than one channel. In Photoshop, it most often refers to a grayscale image with more than one channel.

N

neutral density A value which allows all wavelengths of light to be absorbed equally. With a neutral density an image can be lightened or darkened without a shifting of color.

noise A randomly-distributed color and tonal shift amongst pixels, resulting from scanning of photographic source material or the Photoshop Noise filters.

NTSC Acronym for the National Television Standards Committee; refers to the standard colors of video broadcast. NTSC frames have a television resolution of 525 lines.

O

off-line Any equipment which is not directly communicating with the computer and its components.

on-line Any equipment which is directly communicating with the computer and its components.

opacity The opposite of transparent. The level at which light is blocked.

optical disk A specially treated plastic disk into which digital information is embedded by a laser beam. Laser disks and compact disks are examples of optical disks.

output device Any device that can display computer data, from computer monitors to color printers.

P

path A vector-based beziér curve made with the Pen tool that can be edited at any time. It is used to make masks and clipping paths that require very little storage space.

pattern An image that repeats in tiles to form a regular design.

PAL Acronym for Phase Alternating Line. The television broadcast standard of most of western Europe using 625 lines of resolution.

palette The floating window containing the options for the various tools. Also refers to the colors available to be applied to an image or the colors that exist in that image.

pixel Acronym for picture element, the smallest subdivision of a digital image, which has a set of values that describes its color and tonal qualities (See pixel depth). Also used to refer to a single dot or phosphor element on a computer display device.

pixel depth A measurement of how much information is carried in a single pixel.

posterize The process of reducing the number of colors or gray shades in an image.

post script Page description language used to transfer the information of an image to a printing or output device.

process color The system of 4-color printing that describes each color as a mixture of four ink colors: cyan, magenta, yellow and black.

Q

quarter-tone Tonal value of a dot or pixel whose value is approximately halfway between the highlight and midtone values of an image.

quick mask A method of viewing a mask over an image to facilitate adding to subtracting from the mask.

R

radial fill A fill which is projected from the center out in a circular fashion.

RAM Random Access Memory, the part of the computer which stores instructions and information temporarily. Applied to the running of applications and the execution of commands.

raster-based image An image described as an array of pixels. See Bitmap.

rasterize The process of converting vector information to bitmap or raster based.

ray tracing A feature of 3D programs used to accurately create the surfaces of reflective and refractive objects.

real time The amount of time in which an event would actually occur, as opposed to "slow motion." In interactive media, the feature of having immediate response to user intervention and action.

registration marks In printing, marks used to properly align the individual plates.

rendering The process of creating the final detail and color of a 3D computer-generated image.

resample To change the resolution of an image.

resize To change the dimensions of an image.

resolution The number of dots or pixels of an image contained in a given area. It also refers to the number of bits per pixel. In a printer, it refers to the number of dots per inch.

RGB image A three-channel image made up of the additive colors of red, green and blue.

rotoscope To trace onto paper an image which is projected from a piece of film. Also used to describe the act of manipulating, drawing, or painting directly onto individual frames of a film.

S

sample rate The frequency with which a computer takes a data sample. Sampling takes place when scanning or digitizing any media into the computer.

saturation The intensity or the degree of purity of a color.

scanned image An image which has been digitized on a scanner.

scanner An electronic device which digitizes images into the computer.

scratch disk The hard drive volume where the Photoshop temporary files are stored.

screen angles The angles at which halftone screens are set in relation to each other.

screen frequency The density of dots in a halftone screen.

selection A part of an image which has been segregated from the rest for the purpose of modification or duplication.

seps Short for separations.

separations The individual 4-color process films used to make the plates used for CMYK printing.

shadow The darkest values of an image.

sharpening A selective contrast enhancement used to increase contrast between edges in the image, making images sharper and more "in focus;" edges are determined by the degree of contrast between light and dark pixels.

sixteen-bit color Color depth capable of approximately 65,000 colors per pixel.

spacing The distance between the pixels that are affected by each painting and editing tool.

storyboard A series of drawing used to describe a sequence of motion in film or video.

T

Three-quarter-tone Tonal value of a dot or pixel whose value is approximately halfway between the shadow and midtone values of an image.

tolerance A parameter which specifies the color range of pixels to be selected.

transfer function A method of calibration for imagesetting devices to control, or compensate for, dot gain.

trap An overlap which prevents gaps from appearing along the edges of two objects of different colors caused by misalignment of plates in printing.

tritone An image printed with three inks of different colors.

U

undercolor removal (UCR) The technique for reducing the cyan, magenta and yellow inks from the darkest portion of an image and replacing them with black.

V

virtual memory The use of unused hard disk space as RAM for the storage of temporary memory.

vignette The softening of the edges of a selection to create a gradual transition. See feather, fuzziness.

Z

zoom To magnify or reduce an area of an image to see detail.

All the images in this section were created from scratch, without the use of scans, using Adobe Illustrator and Adobe Photoshop.

Shortcuts

There are many shortcuts in Photoshop for accessing tools and their functions. Here is a short list of some of the most often used.

Tool and all other palettes

Make disappear	Tab
Reappear	Tab
Shrink palette to title bar	Double-click title
Enlarge palette	Double-click title

Tools

Precision crosshair cursor	Cap Lock
Temporary Hand tool	Space bar
Eyedropper tool	Option

(while using another tool which uses color)

Eyedropper tool (with the Eyedropper tool selected)
Select Background color . . . . .Option

Magnifying Glass tool (while using another tool)

Magnify view	Command/Space bar
Reduce Magnification	Command/Space bar/Option
Fit in window	Double-click Hand tool
1:1 ratio	Double-click Magnifying Glass tool

Note: 1:1 is not a dimensional size relation. It refers to the size of the pixels in the image to the resolution of the monitor.

Eraser

Erase to last version saved	Option

Path tool

Add point	Control
Delete point	Control (while cursor is over the point to be deleted)
Temporary Pointer	Command

Sharpen/Blue

Switch between tools	Option-click tool in palette

Dodge/Burn/Desaturate

Switch between tools	Option-click tool in palette

Smudge tool

Temporary Finger painting mode	Option-click and drag

Selection

Switch between

Rectangle and Elliptical marquee	Option-click tool in palette
Add to selection	Shift-click and drag
Subtract from selection	Command-click and drag

Note: different tools can be used in the process of adding and subtracting from a selected area.

Make a copy selected area	Option-click and drag
Move selection marquee drag selection marquee	Option/Command-click and
Constrain selection to square or circle	Shift
Select from center out	Option
Fill selected area with foreground color	Option/Delete
Lasso tool in straight line mode	Option-click

Dialog boxes

Restore original setting	Option-click Reset
Highlight next field	Tab
Highlight previous field	Shift/Tab

Color palette

Delete a color	Command-click color
Replace a color replaced	Option-click color to be
Insert new color between two colors	Option/Shift-click

Print preview

Print preview	Option-click and hold on

Size box on lower left of document window

Resources

All photographic images throughout the book are taken from the PhotoDisc collection.

PhotoDisc, Inc.

2013 Fourth Avenue
Seattle, Washington 98121

(800) 528-3472
(206) 441-9355
(206) 441-9379 Fax

Index

A

Adobe Illustrator
    creating images   118-119
    creating templates   58-61
    importing files   98
    inline text effects   96
Adobe Premiere, alpha channel   39
Airbrush tool   29, 111, 118-119
alpha channel
    changing size   66-67
    choking and spreading   66-67
    creating   34-35, 39-41, 51, 84, 113
    cut-out effect   46-49
    grid creation   50-53
    mask concept   38, 65
    radial gradients   39
    reflection fade   114-115
    saving   17, 19, 24, 103
    storage   39-40
Arbitrary Map   89
Auto Levels   91

B

background layer   69
    colorizing   14-15
    enlargement   50, 110
    retouching   78-79
Bitmap   58, 60
blurring   (see Gaussian Blur)
Brightness/Contrast   89-90
brush shortcuts   74
building created with patterns   62-65
Burn tool   120
buttons, 3D   106-109

C

canvas   (see background layer)
celestial scene
    planet depth   43-44
    planet rings   45
channel
    alpha   (see alpha channel)
    duplication   55
    tones   54-55
Channels palette   3
Choking   (see Minimum filters)
Circular Marquee tool   106, 108
Clipping toggle   91
cloning
    image creation   11-12

restoration   11
retouching   10
color
    adding depth   111-112
    Auto Levels   91
    balance   87, 90
    complementary thumbnail views   94-95
    correction using Image Menu   89-91
    correction using Variation tool   93-95
    edge enhancement   66-67
    falloff color   33
    gradient   (see Gradient tool)
    hue/saturation defined   90
    light source   33
    overlay-neutral color   87
    previews   95
    rainbow blend   72-74
    Range command   91
    reflection color   25, 36
    saturation   54, 90
    selection   17, 46-47, 62, 73, 99-100
    Selective Color   91
    text glow   69
colorizing   17-18
    composite elements   79
    embossed type   105
    grayscale   13-15
    LED effect   108
Colors palette   19
Commands palette   5
compositing
    edge enhancement   66-67
    use of layers   75-79
Constrained Aspect Ratio   108
contrast   28, 89, 90
Crystallize filter   21
Curve controls   92
    for brightness/contrast   89-90
    for inline type effects   97
cutouts   (see alpha channels)

D

defringing   67
depth   43-44, 111-113
desaturation   91, 120
Diffusion Dither   58
drop shadows   80-81

E

edge
    coloring   100
    creating   100
    enhancement   66-67

softening   120 (see also Gaussian Blur filter)
Elliptical Marquee tool   16, 19, 45, 116-117
embossing   69, 103-105
    3D effect   106-107
Eraser tool   74, 78, 85
Eyedropper tool   89

F

Fade option   102
fading, reflection   114-115
Feather command   109
filters   (see names of specific filters)
Find Edges filter   22-23

G

Gaussian Blur filter   44, 48, 67, 74, 77-78, 85, 96
    3D effect   106-107
    embossing   69, 104
    shadows   81
glory shot   110-117
Gradient tool   17, 19, 70, 73
    LED effect   108
    metallic effect   99-101
    shadows   84
    grid creation   50-53

H

hair selection   54-57
histogram   89
hue   90

I

Illustrator   (see Adobe Illustrator)
image
    copying   (see cloning)
    creation   (see painting)
    distortion   52-53, 110-111
    separation   54-57
Inline type effects   96-97
interactive animation program, 3D buttons   106-109
Invert command   23

L

Lasso tool   98-99, 106, 113-114
Layers palette   4, 69-71
layers
    clipped   74
    complex shadows   82-85
    copying   76, 80
    creating   30-31, 62, 72, 76, 86
    drop shadows   80-81
    flattening   71, 101
    global adjustments   86-87

merging   71
moving   81
options   68
overexposure correction   92
parameters   68
retouching   75-79
tricks   71
LED effect   108-109
Lens Flare filter   30-31
Levels   92
   for brightness/contrast   89-90
   for depth   113
   for embossing   105
lighting
   LED effect   109
   light source reflection   116
   Lighting Effect filter   32-37, 57
lightness   90
Line tool grid creation   51-52
logotype creation   58-59

M
marbleizing   23
marching ants (selection marquee)   35-36, 45
masking   (see alpha channels)
Maximum filters   66
Median filter   22
memory
   Disk Cache setup   7
   layers usage   68
Mezotint filter   23
Minimum filters   66
mood, Lighting Effects filter   32-37, 57
Motion Blur filter   26-28
Move tool   78, 81, 88
Multiply application mode   81, 92

N
Noise filter   21-23, 27, 70, 112, 120

O
Offset filter   44, 48
opacity
   adjustment   92, 116
   colorizing grayscale   14
   reflection   25
   transparency effect   20
outlining   75-76, 82
overexposure correction   92
overlays   86-88

P
painting   118-123

palettes   2-5 (see also under names of specific palettes)
Paste Behind option   20
Paste Controls   (see Composite Controls)
Paste Layer option   20
Path tool
   outlining   75-76, 82
   reflection   35-36
   selecting   36, 82-83
Paths palette   4
patterns   62-65
Pen tool   60
performance optimization   6-9
Planet rings   43-45
Premiere   (see Adobe Premiere)
Preserve Luminosity   90
Preserve Transparency   81, 83-84
processor performance   6-7

R
rainbow blend   72-74
RAMDoubler utility   9
Rectangular Marquee tool   18-20, 24-25, 45, 77, 103, 106, 117
reflection
   creating   114
   light source   116
   path   35-36
   water   24-29
Remove Black Matte   67
Remove White Matte   67
Repeat Edge Pixels   44, 48
Replace Color   91
restoration   11
retouching   10, 75-79
Rubber Stamp tool   10

S
Saving a selection   47-49
scanning art   58
scratch disk   6, 68
screening
   colors   72
   with black and white   30
shadows
   complex shadows   82-85
   creating   77-78
   dimensionality   121
   drop shadows   80-81
Sharpen More filter   23
Shear filter   73
Skew option   114
sparkle effect   102
special effects
   3D effects   106-107

cut-out effect   46-49
embossing effects   103-105
inline text   96-97
LED effect   108-109
metallic type   98-102
sparkle effect   102
spotlight   116-117
wet glass effect   88
Spreading   (see Maximum filters)
stone plate, 3D   112-113

T
templates
   drawing detail   59-61
   scanning images   58-59
text   (see type)
texture
   cloning   10, 12
   creating   21-23
   stone   64, 112-113
   wood   119-120
thumbnail views
   color correction   94-95
   memory usage   8
tools   (see names of specific tools)
transparency effect   16-20, 77
type
   blurring   96
   color text glow   69
   creating   47, 96
   embossing effect   69
   inline type effects   96-97
   logotype creation   58-59
   main text mask   69

V
Variations tool   93-95

W
water effect
   cloning   10
   motion   26-28
   reflection   24-29
   texture   23
wet glass effect   88
windows for building pattern   63-64
WindowShade   9
wood texture   119-120

About the Authors

Bert Monroy was born and raised in New York City where he spent 20 years in the advertising industry. He embraced the computer as an artistic medium and is considered one of the pioneers of digital art. Bert is also considered one of the founders of the Multimedia industry with credits dating back before the industry had a title. His photorealistic style is used by a variety of clients, including Industrial Light and Magic and Pacific Data Images. Bert's work has been seen in *MacWorld, MacUser, Byte, Verbum, MacWeek,* to mention a few. His work has also been featured in scores of books which include *Making Art on a Macintosh, The Photoshop WOW Book, The Art of Digital Painting* and *The Grey Book.* His work was also used to introduce many software products such as PixelPaint and ImageStudio. He has written chapters for many books on digital art. Bert is an accomplished teacher and lecturer who has served on the faculty of The School of Visual Arts (NY), Kodak Center for Creative Imaging (ME), Dynamic Graphics Educational Foundation (IL), California College of Arts & Crafts (CA) and SFSU (San Francisco State University). He also lectures at many institutions and trade shows throughout the world. Bert has recently moved his studio from New York City to the San Francisco Bay Area. There he and David Biedny have set up a full service multimedia production studio handling interactive as well as linear presentations.

David Biedny is a leading digital effects and multimedia designer. His writing, multimedia and special effects work have enjoyed global exposure. Working at Industrial Light and Magic, he produced digital effects for movies including *Terminator 2, The Rocketeer, Memoirs of an Invisible Man* and *Hook.* Biedny was formerly president of Incredible Interactivity, where he and his partner Bert Monroy created multimedia projects and products for companies such as General Motors, Knoll International, American Express, the American International Group and AT&T. Biedny was a founding editor of *MacUser* and *Macintosh Today,* is currently a Contributing Editor for *MacUser, New Media, The Macromedia User Journal* and *Morph's Outpost on the Digital Frontier,* and has writtten for *MacWorld, MacWeek,* and *Computer Graphics World,* among others. He coauthored (with Bert Monroy) *The Official Adobe Photoshop Handbook,* originally published by Bantam. Biedny taught Interactive Multimedia Design for the Masters Program of the School of Visual Arts in Manhattan, and has been a top-rated lecturer and speaker at the Kodak Center for Creative Imaging, Seybold Seminars, Pratt, Stanford University, San Francisco State University, MacWorld and NCGA, among others.